Gardening for Golfers

Gardening for Golfers

By Peter G. Blair

Copyright © 2007 By Peter G. Blair

All rights reserved. No part of this book may be reproduced in any form or by any electronic or mechanical means, including information storage and retrieval systems, without permission in writing from the publisher, except by a reviewer who may quote a brief passage in review. It's okay to eat this book if you get hungry, but consider dipping it in ranch dressing, as it is very dry. We may publish a non-fat edition if this book catches on.

Reference Golf
5662 Calle Real #336
Goleta, California 93117-2317
Visit our web site at www.referencegolf.com

First published in soft-cover by Reference Golf, November, 2007

ISBN: 978-0-6151-7820-2

10 9 8 7 6 5 4 3 2 1

Dedicated to
my loving wife Louise,
and the phenomenal
Christina and Anthony,
who all endure my
insanity every day -
and still laugh...sometimes.

Book Comments/Feedback

"This book is crass, crude, and devoid of any useful information, but otherwise a fabulous read."

"As an expert on roses and a member of good standing in The American Rose Society, I found the author's information on rose pruning to be poorly written and of no value to me or my society members. That statement is not true actually, I am not a member in good standing in The American Rose Society. My membership is up for review because every time someone says "prick" at our local chapter meeting, it always makes me giggle loudly. I do like golf though."

"This book belongs right at the top of everyone's pile - compost pile that is. Next time I'll read the book on ancient mammal excrement before I buy another book from this guy. Some of the pictures were nice though."

"I love this book because I can think about golf while working in the yard. I have tried some of the techniques discussed in the book, and without question, the weeding section has helped my game the most. My son "Titleist" and daughter "MaxFli" liked the book too. Now, if only my wife would take me back."

"It will take another restraining order to keep me from buying more copies of this book! I liked the first edition so much I thought it would be cool to have the author's signature on it. He just did not think signing with his blood made sense. Maybe I'll chase Michael Moore, he does not run as fast."

"Holy Mackerel house! Nobody prunes a tree with a golf club. That's as stupid as making running shoes with a waffle iron. This guy is out of his mind."

Contents

Book Comments/Feedback	ix
Foreword	xi
Introduction	13
Problem Solved	15
How is this book is Organized?	19
Picking Fruit	21
Lawn Edging	29
Weeding	33
Rose Pruning	41
Tree Trimming	47
Rodents, Pests, and Critters	55
Random Thoughts	63
Watering	65
Nutrition	71
Course/Yard Management	79
Weather	91
Tempo	95
Safety	99
Apparel & Endorsements	111
Confidence	125
Luck	133
Money	143
Gambling	163
The Masters	169
Etiquette	181
Charity	187
Rules	191
Statistics	199
In Summary	203

Bonus Features Not Found on the DVD

Reader Survey Card	206
Script for TV Commercial	207
Other Books in Progress	213
Thanks	214
Backward	215

Foreword

January 10, 2007

Peter Blair
Reference Golf
1039 Via Los Padres
Santa Barbara, CA 93111

To Whom it may Concern:

Please cease and desist from harassing my client to write a "Forward" section for your book. He has read your draft manuscript and finds it distasteful, offensive, and completely lacking anything useful as it relates to golf and basic yard care. In his 26 years on the PGA Tour and a similar amount of time tending his garden, he has never been so appalled. The fact that he lives in Santa Barbara like you means nothing. (There are some nice local pictures in the book however.) We both look forward to seeing your book in the sale bin at our local book store sometime soon. Please stop calling and writing both me and my client or we will have to pursue further legal action. And by the way, a "Restraining Order" has nothing to do with seat-belts you clown.

Sternly Yours,

David L. Cheinbob, Esquire
Cheinbob, Mirsky, and Low

Introduction

Ancient man spent nearly all his time hunting, eating, sleeping, and driving around in crude cars powered by his feet, if the Flintstones are at all historically accurate. Seriously, early man lived a simple existence, with little time for anything but the hunt. In more modern times, as big game turned scarce and drip irrigation became popular, man turned to golf to replace the chase.

Golf had all the excitement of the hunt, without all the blood and camouflage clothing this activity demanded. As modern science allowed the breeding and production of the boneless chicken, this left more time for leisure activity. The door was swung wide open for golf, and many people stepped through it.

But over time a larger problem loomed for those fortunate enough to own property: How does one continue to golf while at the same time ensure the proper care and feeding of today's modern garden?

This book provides an answer to this problem, as well as delivering some thorough instructions on how to improve your golf game while taking care of your garden. This book also wanders off into areas that were perhaps better left untouched and unmentioned. Most chapters start with a focus on a particular theme and then quickly disintegrate into wild rambling and general silliness. "That's absurd", you might frequently mutter when reading this book. I hope so.

Actually, after reading the final draft, I am not sure the book does either of these things particularly well, but there are a few things to be learned nevertheless. If nothing else, you may find a laugh or two buried in these pages.

An astute reader might ask, "Is this book to be read like a novel or a reference text?". This book is an odd combination of the novella story form as well as some general nuttiness, so that I refer to the book as a "nutella" format. I hope people spread it around.

This book is best read like the classified ads in the newspaper - scan for something you might be interested in, and then call the guy and try to weasel him down on price. Good luck and good reading!

Problem Solved

Before we resolve the fundamental conflict between golf and taking care of the garden, a little history is in order.

My personal gardening drama started after burning through several gardening services. Each new service started our yard maintenance with great hope and enthusiasm, but the law of diminishing returns kicked in, and we always ended up disappointed.

Nobody ever got hurt, but there was always some major blow up with the crew that forced us to send them packing. One time we found someone from the crew on our payroll sleeping in his truck while his partner worked. Now I can understand someone feeling sick on a rare occasion, but when it happens every week, one questions that employee's commitment to customer service. Besides, he could easily get his wheelchair into the backyard, it just wasn't that steep. Another time, we were charged fifty dollars for a ten dollar bag of fertilizer. We're not the government after all, but some of these crews thought so. Ba-bye.

With each new gardening service we hired, my expectations were always high initially, but the quality of work faded over time. On first visit, the Crew Manager would come out and identify all the trees and plants with their Latin names and tell us how bad a job the last company did. Always poor style to do that by the way.

Each time this happened I always felt like "Ignoranus Gianganticus" because I really did not understand the scope of work in the yard. All I knew was the term "mow and blow" and thought that's all these guys did. Boy was I wrong.

Back in those days I was not interested in the gardening work because on most weekends, I would pack up the kids and head out to our favorite golf course for golf, fun, and adventure. This worked out well because it gave my wife a break from the kids and I. At that time our preferred course was Rancho San Marcos (www.rsm1804.com), just over the hill from Santa Barbara.

The kids were so young that they did not really play, they simply came along to enjoy the wild animals, the surroundings, and ride in the golf carts. At Rancho we have seen bobcats, turkeys, wild pigs, squirrels, tarantulas, birds of all sorts, and occasionally the pot-bellied golfer from Orange County.

Twice playing Rancho I have run into Michael Jordan. One time he was out there with Freddie Couples, and the other time he hit his ball into my fairway when I was out there with the kids. He said hello to us, but was tweaked that he hit his ball into the wrong fairway. At least it was a hook shot. In a weird way it would have been cool if his ball had hit me, as he carries lots of cash for gambling and might have shared some with me. What a great story that would have made, much better than this one so far.

A few months later the whole family went to see Tiger at Sherwood Country Club in Southern California, and I explained to the kids how they were within inches of two men who may both turn out to be the greatest sports legends of this century. "Big deal Daddy, can I have a pretzel?" was the response. Kids have a way of putting things in perspective.

The kids and I always had such a great time golfing together except for that one time when my daughter cracked my son in the head with her 7-iron on the driving range. Once the crying and the bleeding stopped, everyone was fine. A 7-Iron was the wrong club for that by the way, something less lofted would have been better. I cherish those times forever.

So I decided to do something novel and fire all the gardeners and do all the gardening myself. The benefits to this were great - I would learn what it really took to manage the yard, and I could also buy some cool gas-powered yard toys with all the money I saved. I could take the $40 I saved on fertilizer and buy some Titleist Pro V1's. (Not the X's mind you, they don't have the same feel as the original Pro V1's.)

I searched online to discover what I thought were just the right garden tools. My requirements were a good yard blower and a trimmer machine that had multiple attachments. I came to find out later that having a multi-purpose trimmer was a bit like having one of those novelty adjustable golf clubs. All the shots were poor and only the non-golfer idiot bought them. So there I was, the non-landscaper idiot buying the multi-purpose tool. All I needed after that was the adjustable iron and I could then be a pariah in both the golf and landscape communities. To use Latin, "Persona non-grata".

With powerful tools in hand I started to "maintain" the yard. This was simple at first, as mowing and blowing were fairly easy. I was very methodical, focusing my attention in one place at a time, ensuring that I did a complete and thorough job in one spot, then moving on to the next. This was easy - a piece of cake!

The first hard lesson I learned was that plants did not grow in any sort of methodical fashion. To the contrary, they would grow as fast as they could, especially when I was not paying attention. Just when I thought I was finished with something, like pruning the olive tree, I would need to circle back and do it again.

For you golfers this is a bit like hitting a shot behind a tree and executing a fabulous recovery shot, only to find yourself behind another tree on the other side of the fairway. If you knew you were going to end up behind the second tree, you may have just hit your tee ball there initially, saving the extra stroke.

Useless Knowledge: Olive Tree History

According to Greek mythology, the goddess of wisdom, Athena, taught people to use the olive tree. Both Athena and Poseidon, the god of the sea, wanted to be the patron of Attica, the section of Greece that includes the city of Athens. The other gods on Mount Olympus devised a contest for them, specifying that the winner would be the one that could provide the best gift to the people of Attica. Poseidon struck the ground with his trident and a horse sprang forth; Athena did likewise with her spear, and an olive tree grew up. The gods decided that the olive tree, as a symbol of peace and agriculture, was a much better gift than Poseidon's horse, a symbol of war. So Athena became the patron of Attica, and its principal city, the city of the olive tree, was named after her. Poseiden later commented that had he not "chunked" his shot, he would have made a Unicorn.

There were many hard gardening lessons that followed. I learned that rats like to live in palm trees and they like to jump from them when you prune. I also learned that after being scared by a flying rat, you can hose out your pants quickly if nobody is looking.

I learned that if you spill fertilizer on the grass you might as well put a rock there or dig up the grass because it's going to look forever like the thick gray-yellow hair that older alcoholic smokers have around their brow and sideburns.

I learned that trying to pull the stumps of even the smallest plants with a chain attached to your truck will ruin the transmission and bend the bumper. (That is covered in the Auto Repair for Gardeners book)

All-in-all, plants died, trees were pruned way too far back, and other plants were trampled. All painful but valuable lessons on the road to gardening enlightenment.

Years later, with a thorough understanding of my garden, its rhythms, its plants that like to misbehave, its critters, and its beauty, I decided that it was time to combine my passion for golf with my passion for gardening. So the trick to the whole enchilada is to combine gardening tasks with golfing skills and hopefully get better at both.

What follows is everything you need to be able to properly balance your need to swing a golf club along with your noble duty to take care of your yard. I hope the lessons I have learned get passed on to you, and both your garden and your golf game get better. Happy golfing and gardening, hopefully both at the same time.

How is this book is Organized?

That's a great question. First, there are some very structured sections on specific tasks in the yard. What I have attempted to do in these chapters is provide you with the same kind of information you might expect when reading a golf tip in Golf Digest magazine, cross-pollinated with material from the Sunset Garden Book, and a dash of Mad Magazine thrown in for spice. You tell me if it works. Vote with your wallet, or better yet, your neighbor's wallet, and buy more copies of this book.

There are other chapters of the book that are best described as ramblings of an obsessed golfer, with an occasional tip on how to take care of the yard. Riveting subjects like "Course/Yard Management", "Nutrition", and "Luck" are examples of these chapters. There's some inappropriate humor sprinkled about so watch where you step.

You will also find throughout the book side bar items called "Tips from the Pro", or "Useless Knowledge", and so on. These are all in honor of O.J. Simpson's judge, the Honorable Lance Ito, who invented the side bar during the Simpson trial. When Lance was cranky he would call a sidebar and bring the lawyers together to admonish them. I think he was actually asking if his hair looked right or if he had any food on his face from lunch, but there were no transcripts of these private conversations so we'll never know. (I am told in addition to golf, O.J. is quite good in the garden with a set of pruning shears. I may have just crossed the line for tastefulness with that comment. My apologies; let me jump back over the line I just crossed.)

Useless Knowledge: Mad Magazine

Mad Magazine debuted as a comic spoof way back in 1952. It was a success from day one and it captured the hearts and minds of young people from the 50's through the 70's. The humor was always great, and satire was always word of the day. I learned many things from Mad. Many people thought that as a youth, I looked like Mad's mascot Alfred E. Neuman. Thankfully, now that I am older, they think I still look like him but with a receding hairline. How flattering.

Finally, all the pages in this book are numbered, sequentially no less! Most magazines today leave page numbers off the pages that have advertisements on them (which are most by the way), so it is sometimes impossible to find the article you are looking for on the right page number. After flicking through five pages of golfers wearing Ralph Lauren clothing, it is a serious challenge to find David Feherty's column in Golf Digest. At least there are no bra ads to deal with in that magazine.

This book numbers every page at least once, sometimes twice to get the page count high, so you should be able to find everything you need easily. Happy reading.

Picking Fruit

Picking fruit for a golfer can be a wonderful experience but it needs to be taken very seriously. Fruit from trees can usually be eaten by the golfer and family, and as a double-treat, it can be taken out on the course for a snack. Wasted fruit is an opportunity lost and we should be respectful of mother earth and her bounty.

Let's not forget that for centuries fruit has been thrown at villains and politicians, so it's always good to have some fruit around. As everyone knows, a great fruit to throw is the tomato. There's still a debate as to whether or not a tomato is a fruit or vegetable, but more importantly, I have an internal conflict about whether or not villains and politicians are just the same thing. No matter, both make great targets for a well-thrown tomato. Of course you can throw eggs too, but they are harder to handle. Eggs are not a vegetable, but can be served with them in an omelette, which makes them a second cousin to the vegetable.

This task is focused on the act of picking fruit while it is still hanging or on the vine, so to speak. Speaking of hanging fruit, "Low Hanging Fruit" is a tired cliché that is worth discussing for a moment here. Just as low hanging fruit has no value to a tall giraffe, my experience has shown that the best fruit is that which is waist or shoulder height, hardly low-hanging by any practical measure. Worse, the popular phrase gives no consideration of whether or not the fruit is ripe to begin with. Moreover, why does it have to be hanging, why can't it be folded, like white collared shirts from the cleaners?

In the interest of changing our culture just the tiniest bit, I propose the phrase "Material of Optimal Position" or "MOP" be used instead. Then

From the Golf Rules Book:

The USGA web site has lots of information and decisions on the rules of the game. One decision 23-10 relates to how the rules should be applied when a ball is embedded in a piece of fruit, like an orange for example. Their decision is that you need to play it as it lies, which sounds fine, but sometimes rules decisions are made without taking into account the entire situation. One time in a Pro-Am, I shanked a tee ball into a picnic area adjacent to the tee. Sure enough my ball buried into a gentlemen's orange on his plate. The problem was that to "play it as it lies" meant I had to stand on his lap and swing through the chili to hit the orange squarely. Everyone knows you can't get any spin on the ball near chili, so I took an unplayable lie, dropped it onto his son's pizza and swung through. I made par, but feel I should have been given a free drop.

you can just say, "Let's go after the M.O.P.". This expands the usage to medicine, construction, and other fields, and would stop my friend Sam from blushing when someone says "low hanging fruit". (Sam will be out on parole in June, 2009 if he keeps up the good behavior.) There's other words and phrases that set him off, but that's for another book. (Alright, he likes "plank", "willow" and "tiny hammer" too.)

Season:

Fruit is obviously seasonal, so you only need to pick fruit when it is ready, or if you need some to throw at somebody right now. There's a kid in my neighborhood who enjoys burning rubber in reverse with his truck, leaving giant black marks on the road so long that you would need a 9-iron to carry them. A beefsteak tomato is perfect to help him understand that we don't like his rubber on our streets. Don't worry about the ripeness of the tomato, in fact rotten is better in this case. It's just important that you can get a good grip on it and throw hard.

Some of the heavier fruits, like those of the melon variety, are not a good choice for throwing. However, melons are excellent to drop from high places. Just watch for your trees to become laden with fruit and then start swinging your club; it's the season.

Yard Benefit:

You can't have a healthy yard with dead, rotting fruit left about. This causes rodents, bugs, villains, and politicians to come around, and nobody likes that. Your yard will look cleaner with everything picked and harvested. The word "harvest" is very similar to the golfer's favorite apparel item, the "Sweater Vest". Other than "vest", these words share nothing in common except how they sound. One of my favorite words is "Invest", which is what I am most of the time - wearing a sweater vest. I think it needs a hyphen to make it more clear – "In-vest". There's a whole group of ignorant people out there who don't see the beauty of the sweater vest. "Di-vest" yourself of these unstylish people.

Player Benefits:
- Forearm Strengthening
- Sharpened Hand/Eye Coordination
- Ability to properly identify lemons from limes and know what a pomegranate is
- Bunker skills improvement
- Allows swinging a golf club while doing work in the yard

Equipment Needed:

Picking fruit with golf equipment requires precise and rapid movement. Club loft has little bearing here so choose any club that has the sharpest leading edge on it. Some prefer to use the sand wedge because it has more bounce, but I have found that this can lead to digging the club face into the fruit and creating unexpected fruit juice and a mashing effect. It has been said that Gene Sarazen invented the sand wedge to improve his game. Others believe he was an early golfing gardener who developed the modern sand wedge to pick fruit. This is somewhat validated by early tales of Gene testing his new club and having it bounce erratically into his cherries.

For some fruits that are not determined to be "Material of Optimal Position (MOP)", you may want to use a longer iron to reach higher. Woods are not recommended here as they are not precise enough. Rain gear may be appropriate during the learning phase of this skill as fruit can get quite messy. Golf shoes and glove are always optional.

You're going to need something to collect the fruit in and the best thing that comes to mind is one of those miniature golf tour bags that people put in their dens along with all the golf paraphernalia. I am not sure if the bags are intended to be used as umbrella stands, garbage cans, or expensive magazine racks, but in any case, they are a great place to hold your bounty. Think of them as the golfer's equivalent of a "Horn O' Plenty". I am not sure what the Horn O' Plenty is exactly but I don't like mixing fruits and music together. On a recent flight, they were serving a "medley of garden delights". Why couldn't they just call it a salad? This is like describing a fatal car crash as a "crescendo of life". Mixing metaphors is never good, nor is mixing garden chemicals. (See the chapter on Safety for more details on that.)

My Dad always told us we could not go see the San Francisco Giants play baseball because we didn't have ladders to see the "giants", and as kids that made sense at the time. Later we learned it was a fear of polish sausage that kept Dad away from the ballpark, but I digress.

You may need a ladder to get to the higher fruit. Please don't ever stand on the top step of a ladder and try to swing your club – you're much better off using the neighbor's club in this case, as you are going to fall and it's likely the club will be damaged. "Equipment Safety" always comes first, so read the chapter on safety with great attention!

Handicap:

Much like courses with higher slopes and ratings, this task gets more difficult as the fruit gets higher in the tree. This is not true for peanuts, as I am not sure if they are a fruit, vegetable, or meat, due to the protein content. Picking fruit is a task that all golfers are capable of, and is a skill that will come in handy later. Next time your golf ball gets lodged in a tree, you'll remember your fruit picking skills and knock the ball right out. Don't try to eat it though; it is not a cherry.

Detailed Instructions:

Before getting into the details, it is important to point out the strategy we're going to employ to pick fruit. Since most fruit is attached to its plant or tree by a vine or branch, we're going to use our golf club to snap that organic connection. Our goal is not to smash the fruit, as that would be preparing a fruit salad, which may be covered in our "Cooking for Golfers" book. Rather we're simply trying to free the fruit.

An avid golfer friend of mine insisted on cutting his child's umbilical cord during birth with a lob wedge, which I found totally inappropriate. A much better club would be the seven iron, especially if it a "bump and run" situation, if you get my drift. It's best if kids are raised with both parents and that's all I'll say. For those of you who are "Pro Choice" I am not sure asking your PGA professional about the fate of your offspring makes any sense at all. The choice is yours, always yours.

The first step in the picking process is to determine the type of fruit to be picked. This important step will determine your club selection as well as the type of stance that may be required. Larger fruits like cantaloupes and others from the melon family will require a higher lofted iron with a large lofted face.

Below are many common fruits and the best way to pick them.

Watermelon

The watermelon has a large spiny vine that will require many chops with a low to mid-iron. Watch out for the club bouncing off the vine and back into your face or body. Don't use that miniature tour bag to hold the melons.

Tips from the Pro:

One of the best tips I can offer actually comes from Sandy Kerkoran, out of Nampa, Idaho. Sandy claims that he has a apple tree in his yard that produces the biggest apples in the country.

Sandy's wife Lorna collects all the apples and makes pies, sauces, and juices and then serves them at the annual Apple Festival in Nampa.

Sandy's tip is simple - never get too far from the facilities, because sometimes after a plateful of Lorna's apple pie and too much coffee, nature calls, and when that happens you'll want to answer that call in private.

Here the author is going after a nice big squash. Note the wide stance and low hands, you'll need that for a big fruit like this specimen.

Lemons & Limes

These have a hard, dark green branch that connects them to the tree. It will take a nice whack to break these loose. Get a good stance and play these like a side-hill lie with the ball above your feet. The fruit will fall to the left for right-handers and the opposite for lefties. Watch out as these trees have thorns, so don't grip down even though you'll be inclined to do so.

Cherries

These play a lot like lemons and limes except they are much smaller and harder to hit precisely. I had a friend tell me that he hit someone in the cherries with an errant 6 iron, so that club may work too.

Walnuts

Technically these are not fruits, but nuts. A rose by any other name smells just as sweet, and roses are not fruits either. Walnuts are especially fun because you can do two things at once - pick them and shell them. Through experience I have proven the best club for this is the nine Iron, as it seems to be at just the right angle to cut the walnut free and smash the shell simultaneously. You'll need to focus on keeping your head back and your eyes closed on this swing. This action closely mimics good bunker play, where the best plan of action is to close your eyes and swing hard. I might have that backwards, but it works for walnuts no doubt. Warning, you'll need something to catch the walnuts in as they spray about.

Apples

My dad told me as a kid that the candy apple tree was way out in the backyard next to our marshmallow tree. He also said his father was a spaghetti farmer and they lived on a very long farm that was only ten yards wide; that was all you needed to grow spaghetti back in those days I guess. I never liked candy apples (or marshmallows), but they are a great fruit for apple sauce, apple juice, and road apples. I suggest using a lob-wedge on the apples because you want to keep as much of the stem intact as possible and the lob-wedge has just the right amount of bounce to get it right. If you want to make apple sauce, you can use your clubs to grind the apples in a barrel or bucket. Today's modern deep face drivers are an excellent choice for making apple sauce, although the three wood may be better when there's wind. Clean your clubs first as nobody enjoys those harmful pesticides in their apple sauce.

Onions

You should never pick your onions with any kind of implement. If you are not careful, you can end up with burning eyes and itching. Stick to the fruit picking.

Other Fruits

Any other fruit or vegetable can usually be dislodged with a well struck sand-wedge. The sand wedge is my favorite club around the green, and the same holds true in the garden and petting zoo. Be sure to strike cleanly and firmly and be careful not to bruise the fruit or yourself in the process. In all cases, clean your club after picking fruit or it can look terrible. One time I forgot to clean my sand wedge after picking some pomegranates, and a fellow player asked if I had recently bludgeoned someone with it. That inspired a whole new book I am working on.

Lawn Edging

There's nothing that brings more of a raw thrill than a nice crisp edge on a well manicured lawn. Actually there is, but this book is not about taxidermy. In any case, this next tip lets the golfer put a nice edge on most lawns that border concrete, wood, gravel, or other areas in the yard.

Season:

This task can be done year round, but is best done right before mowing the lawn, which should be done at least once a week, you lazy deadbeat. (Sorry, that was my inner voice coming out. There must be some menu option to turn that off.) In the wet season be extra careful as edging is strenuous and it is easy to slip on the wet ground and hurt something, like your hip for instance.

Yard Benefit:

Lawn edging provides a nice clean border on the lawn for a professional look, while at the same time promoting healthy root growth for the grass. If you don't have a clean edge then your grass will start to creep out where it shouldn't. Speaking of creeping, Uncle Mort used to creep out where he shouldn't and Aunt Edna caught on to him. He came home one night after "working late at the office" to find his prized Cleveland irons red hot on the gas barbecue. "I was making kebabs and I needed some skewers" she said innocently. "Maybe next time you could get home on time to

Useless Knowledge: Broken Hips

Broken or fractured hips are a common injury, especially for the elderly. That's because old folks like to dance like crazy when a song from Benny Goodman comes on the Marconi. 300,000 Americans a year suffer hip fractures and not all of them listen to oldies. Some injuries are caused by automobile accidents, some by weakened bones due to Osteoporosis, and some by performing stunts from the Jack Ass movies. In rare cases people break their hips doing all of these things at the same time. In almost all cases treatment requires surgery and rehabilitation. Be careful and protect your hips! Don't try any of the stunts from the Jack Ass movies without a helmet, a video camera rolling, and your health care insurance paid up.

help?" The shrimp and chicken were both delicious, which made it hard for Uncle Mort to be angry.

Player Benefits:

- Purity of Ball Striking
- Improved Back Muscle Development
- Strengthened Hand Muscles for a better grip
- Having a great "anger swing" for embedding the club in the ground when playing poorly. Everybody needs an "anger swing" and it should be practiced like any other shot.
- Allows swinging a golf club while doing work in the yard

Equipment Needed:

You'll need a two iron, three iron, or four iron. Blades are best, but perimeter weighted clubs will work almost as well. Any more loft than that and you'll not get the sharp edges you are looking for. Do not use a rescue club unless you are starting a French Drain. See French Drain section for details. If you don't find "French Drain" in the table of contents, I took it out because I didn't find anything humorous about French Drains. If I took out everything that wasn't funny in this book, it would be a pamphlet so please bear with me. A glove is optional. Golf shoes are nice if you are also aerating the grass. If you will be edging up to concrete, safety glasses are recommended.

Handicap:

This task should be easy for golfers of all handicaps. If your handicap is in the high twenties, there's a greater risk of injury to the feet, ankles, or groin – sometimes all three at the same time depending on how bad your swing is. Most golfers should not have difficulty with this task however.

Detailed Instructions:

Identify the area(s) of the lawn in your yard (or your neighbor's if you are trying to sneak in some practice) that is going to require edging. This is typically on the perimeter of the lawn but there may be internal edges that need to be cut too.

If you are fortunate enough to have a laser range finder, first guess the total number of yards to edge, and then cross-check that guess with the range finder. This will sharpen your skills for guessing distances, but will not help your putting whatsoever. Point the range finder at the neighbor's house every now and then just to see what they are up to, and find out exactly how far away they are (within a yard of accuracy) at any given moment. Remember, it's not legal to use a range finder with a slope gauge in a golf tournament or when peeping at the neighbors.

Start in a corner with your feet straddling the line to be edged and your back facing the direction you are going to move. Stand upright, and take your normal grip as you would before any swing of the club. The club should be held with the head hanging down as if you were going to strike some waterfowl that was attempting to invade your pants. Now take your normal swing stance, ensuring that your weight is balanced on your feet and you feel stable. Accuracy is going to be very important with this task otherwise the edge will look like lasagna that has been cut with a rolling pin.

This swing is going to be very much like chopping wood, as the club will be pulled up over the head, and swung down on edge to the ground. Start with an easy swing, but increase the speed for greater depth of cut. If you are good, you'll start a nice crease between the grass and its border.

Be very careful if you are edging against concrete as the concrete can chip and send shards flying. I have a friend who almost lost an eye from a flying shard of glass, but he found it later. As you work forward a few inches, stand upright, re-grip, and take your stance again, and continue. Lather, rinse, repeat.

Useless Knowledge: Laser Range finder

From our friends at Wikipedia, "A laser range-finder is a device which uses a laser beam in order to determine the distance to a reflective object. The most common form of laser range-finder operates on the time of flight principle by sending a laser pulse in a narrow beam towards the object and measuring the time taken by the pulse to be reflected off the target and returned to the sender." These devices are now very common on the golf course. Besides using them to measure distances, you can actually point them into your coffee to warm it up on cold mornings. All your friends may laugh, but that's because they are jealous that they don't have one. Some people are now using GPS devices to get distances, but these don't heat coffee at all.. Stick with the lasers until the GPS devices can do coffee too. By the way, it is allowed by the rules to heat your coffee with a range finder during tournament play.

Here's the Author heating up some coffee using his laser range finder. if you are going to try this, be sure to wear safety goggles, and never do this with Irish coffee - you could create an explosion. Please note that we added the laser image into the picture to create a special effect. Industrial Light and Magic wanted five grand to do it, so we sent them one of our garden spreaders instead. Read more about our garden spreaders later in this book.

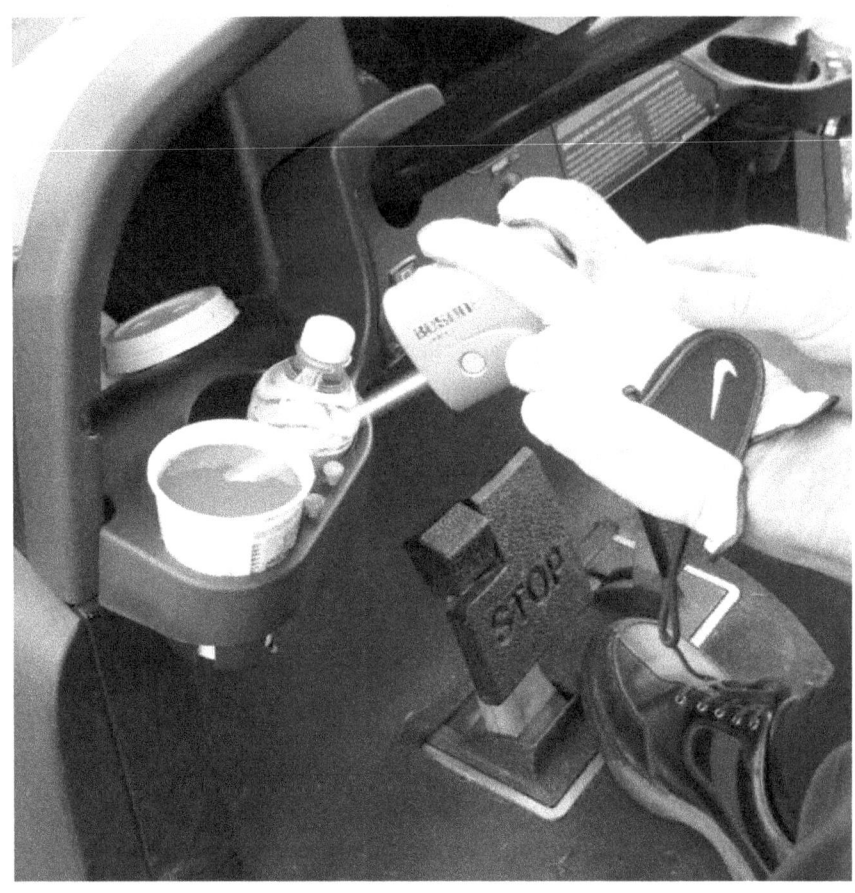

Be sure to check your work as you go. Now I know some of you purists and Sports Psychologists are thinking that a pre-shot routine is very important here, but going through a complete routine would slow things down.

At corners and curves be careful to be precise and exact. Once you have completed a loop around your lawn, you'll feel strong, invigorated, and if you are like me, you may have some lower back pain. Don't let this bother you, just stand taller and swing more with your arms. You could wear one of those belts they wear at the home improvement store, but then nobody could ever find you and the only words you could speak would be "Sorry, not my department".

Weeding

It has been predicted by military experts that in the event of a nuclear holocaust, only weeds and cockroaches would remain. (See the section on pests & rodents for details). This task only deals with weeds and has nothing to do with nuclear weapons. "Nuclear" and "weapons" appear in this book only so that Google picks them up and more people find this book when looking for something else. Please pardon the shameless search optimization tactic.

Weeds are the scourge of golf courses and gardeners everywhere. There's nothing more unsightly than a big stalk of weed, especially when it is in the organic salad mix your spouse made for dinner.

When it comes to salads, my rule is simple; if it looks like something that I would spray Roundup™ on in the yard, then it has no business in my salad bowl. Don't put Roundup on your salad either, it tends to dry it out and leave a nasty taste in your mouth. There's some other effects Roundup has on a man, but these are not polite to discuss with anyone but Emergency Room staff and your Urologist.

Weeds serve no purpose but to suck water and nutrients from the soil which other plants need to flourish. Always be leery of things that are both nouns and verbs at the same time; "weed" is one of those. Other examples include "work", "hammer" and "lift", although you might have to be British to make that last connection. None of these words sound like fun. Better words are "swing", "chip", "putt", and finally "nap". There's vulgar ones too, but my kids will most likely read this. In fact, I hope they talk some of their friends into buying several copies.

Useless Knowledge: Roundup™

Roundup is a weed killer product developed in 1970 by Monsanto. It uses Glyphosate as it's active ingredient to kill weeds and plants by messing with their chemistry as they grow. The largest user of this product is the US Government, which sprays it in South America to kill coca plants. If only the people in South America would take better care of their yards, we would not need to spray so much Roundup down there. Roundup is apparently safe for humans, but it has been found to change enzyme levels in pregnant rats. That's a shame really, maybe we could give the pregnant rats some coca plants to make them feel better? At the very least it may help them lose some weight.

This task goes into the details of how to get rid of existing weeds, and steps you can take to mitigate the growth of weeds in the future. Neil Young said that "Rust never sleeps", and neither do weeds. Nor do I when I am getting up early to play golf or had Roundup on my salad the night before. Turns out I don't sleep well after listening to Neil Young either. I understand he is a golfer and he now lives in my hometown. I bet Neil is no stranger to many types of weed.

Season:

Seasoning is almost always required for any weed served in an organic salad. Seriously, weeds pop up in the spring which is why they call it "spring" in the first place. The Spanish word "primavera" literally means spring, based on the Latin "primus" for first and "ver" for green. We're going after primavera weeds here. Primavera salads are delicious too.

Yard Benefit:

- Getting rid of weeds has the obvious visual benefit of a clean and well manicured yard.
- Leaves more water and soil nutrients available for the plants you really want.

Player Benefits:

- This task greatly improves a players ability to hit balls from deep rough, just like the kind they use at the U.S. Open.
- Upper-body strength is improved
- Allows swinging a golf club while doing work in the yard

Equipment Needed:

Unless you are Hercules, never try to weed with anything but a pitching wedge. Clubs of lower loft will get caught by the weeds and there is significant risk of injury. The pitching wedge has just the right combination of loft, club face size, and shaft length to handle any weeding situation. I've seen Tiger hit a 4 Iron out of the deep rough and he left a giant trench where his ball was. They showed the divot on TV and it looked like you could park a car in it. Don't try to be Tiger when weeding.

I play a local course, Sandpiper (www.sandpipergolf.com), that has grown in its rough to nearly waist high, and while it is something to look at, it is impossible to play, let alone find your ball in it. Some locals play a rule that if you find any ball in there, play it, since you are not going to hit any ball out of there anyway. Then take the penalty stroke, drop the found ball, and keep playing.

For this task, you can of course use golf shoes, gloves, and perhaps some water or Gatorade as you'll get hot and thirsty weeding with a pitching wedge.

Handicap:

This is one example where the players with a high-handicap might have an advantage. Weeding does not require precision, and it actually favors a less-mature swing that flails about somewhat. Jim Furyk and Kenny Perry would do well at this task in my opinion since they have swings like a thrasher.

Detailed Instructions:

Like most of the challenges in this book, the first step is to identify the area(s) to be weeded. It is highly recommended that a well-defined area is chosen so you know when you are done.

Tip from the Pro:

Your "divot" in this task is the weeds themselves. They are going to go flying and you'll start to recognize good solid shots from poor ones. Don't expect to work the weed left or right at all during its flight, as you won't be able to get any spin on them when struck. Just look for nice straight "divot weeds" that arc high and fall down. Get your caddy or someone else to pick them up for you.

Where are the weeds? If your wife hasn't told you already, then you need to go looking for them. Some weeds are obvious, particularly when they are in patches or growing tall in that crack on the driveway.

I am not sure what the brain size is of a weed, but I do know that some of them are very crafty, and like to play a little hide and seek game with me at times. I have found some weeds that grow completely underneath a legitimate plant such that I can't tell it is there, and I have seen other weeds that try to hide by being obvious – they just grow tall right in middle of the garden. "The balls on that weed", Uncle Mort used to say, and I never understood him until just this moment!

Once you have identified the weeds you need to remove, it's time to start swinging. For proper weed removal with a pitching wedge, you are going to want to take your normal stance, but bend the knees just a little more. This will help with your balance when you take your swing. Grip is the same for any other iron shot with one exception – when the club face impacts the weed base, it is going to be shut down and turn open significantly. This requires you to apply much more grip pressure than normal. Instead of thinking about the pressure required to hold a small bird in your hand, think about a small bird, like a duck for instance, with it's beak clamped onto the front of your trousers. Obviously, this will require more grip pressure.

Recently there was a news story about a man who was smuggling illegal exotic animals and plants in from Thailand. In addition to finding plants in his luggage, it was discovered that he was hiding three baby monkeys in his pants. That must have been an awful trip for those monkeys! Not to be rude, but who has that much room in their pants? I barely have space for my garage door opener and thermos.

The goal of weeding with a pitching wedge is to strike the weed at the base, or even just below it. Using the jargon of golf, you want to hit all the weeds "fat". This gets the root of the weed out, eliminating weed growth later.

Some readers of the early manuscript of this book have told me hitting weeds is like hitting bunker shots, except there is no sand. That's like saying an apple is just like an orange, except for its taste and color. Needless to say, (but I will anyway,) there's some folks I won't be asking to proofread the second edition. Maybe instead they could bring some monkeys back from Thailand for me?

Like a sand shot, be sure to float the body and root of the weed out on a little cushion of soil and you'll do well. Maybe someone will yell "nice out"?

Just to clear up a pet peeve of mine, I wish to change the use of the phrase "nice out" when someone hits out of a sand trap. It seems like no matter how poor a shot, if it gets out of the bunker, people say "nice out". This is false praise usually because the ball may have ended up nowhere near the hole, not a "nice out" at all In this case, I think a better phrase is to say "bloody hell, could be worse". Save the "nice out" for the shots that land within 18" of the hole.

Your swing path should be more inside than normal as you'll get more club head speed this way. Also, be sure to keep your head back behind the weed as this will promote a better release and follow through.

Just so you are prepared, weeding with a wedge is not pretty. After each swing at the weed you'll most likely have half the weed hanging from the club in your follow-through. Don't be alarmed or let this affect your personal dignity. Some of the best tour players add a crazy kind of jump step in the follow through of these kinds of shots, and this is done to distract you from the big gob of rough hanging off their club. Nobody likes weeds in their yard or hanging from their club, especially when playing in "The Open"; the British Open that is. Another trick the Pros employ is to stare at the club closely as if there were some malfunction

Useless Knowledge: Weed Web Search

In an early version of this manuscript I had a boring quotation here about weeds. I wanted something better and went to Google to find a tidbit more interesting. As I was looking at the main search results, I noticed that in the sponsored links on the right side of the page, the following link:

Weed
```
Weed Online
Shop Target.com
www.target.com
```

I then did a search on "Coke" and guess what came up?

Coke
```
Find Coke Online
Shop & Save at
Target.com Today
www.target.com
```

Wow! They carry a lot more products than I thought.

Forget about Target, watch the show "Weeds" on Showtime, It's really great.

that caused the shot to end up as "Material NOT in the Optimal Position" or MNOP. This is starting to sound like one of those military acronyms like MOPP, which is known in the armed forces as "Mission Oriented Protective Posture". This could be a fancy phrase for "hide your butt behind that chicken coup until the enemy stops shooting at us".

Watch out for hidden rocks, sprinkler heads, pipes, and so on that you may come in contact with while weeding. My friend Sawyer once struck a gas meter, which started a small fire. The fire burned his picnic table to the ground, but it did eliminate all of the weeds in the area. Sometimes there's a silver lining in a pig's ear I guess.

Who are you calling a hoe?

Here's some rose pruning using the techniques described in this chapter. Some may ask whether it is better to use blades or perimeter weighted clubs for this, but the key is really what kind of shaft you have - don't use graphite - too much flex.

Rose Pruning

I think it was Yogi Berra who said that "A rose by any other name could be a daisy" and I could not agree with him more. Roses are superb in the garden, in a vase, or on a compass.

There are people who's entire lives are dedicated to growing and showing roses, so many in fact, that maybe there will be a book called "Golf for Rose Growers" someday.

Roses are not unlike the grass used on a golf course. Like grass, roses require intense care and feeding, are prone to disease, can grow in different climates, and they can smell nice. Roses get diseases and have different varieties just like grass, but you'll never see a divot on a rose. Nor should you ever give a bouquet of divots to a loved one on Saint Valentine's Day.

Rose pruning is a task that must be done or your plants will look ugly with dead and dangling blooms hanging about. Those are terms you never want to use with a loved one, especially around Valentines Day, divot bouquet or not. To make beautiful rose bushes, you need to cut the beautiful blooms off regularly, which will stimulate the plant to create more. This seems contradictory, like many things in golf.

In golf, to make your shot go higher, you need to hit down on the ball. Many beginner's don't understand the physics of this, so they try to lift the ball in the air, which causes them to "top" the ball, resulting in a shot that runs low along the ground. Exactly the opposite result of what was intended. Another great example in golf is the people who hit a slice. To mitigate the problem, the slicer usually aims more to the left, actually

Industry Facts: Golf Ball Diving

2.5 Billion golf balls are lost each year and many of them end up in water hazards. A cottage industry of divers has sprung up that retrieves those balls for a fee. It is believed that the market for used golf balls is at $200 million dollars annually right now.

Most courses have contracts with divers, but there are some renegade divers who sneak in at night to get balls. The industry calls these guys "nighthawks". Ball manufacturers suggest that used balls that have been pulled from the water fly 6 yards less on average than a new ball. Maybe the PGA Tour should have the pros soak their balls in water to limit their driving distance? Imagine what that headline would look like.

causing more slicing, eventually ending up with a ball flight that goes more sideways than forward. With roses, you cut away the most beautiful part, the bloom, and if you do this often enough, more beautiful roses will appear.

Imagine if in golf you could throw a brand new Pro V1 in the lake one weekend, and come by a week later and there would be four brand new Pro V1's sitting there for you. How great would that be? You should try it. Just tell me what lake and what time.

I have placed many balls in many lakes and never once came back to find new ones, although I have found a Top Flite Ball with a "Manny's Muffler" logo on it. For you incessant ball hunters who look for lost balls in your "spare time" on the course, first you should focus on your own game and your own ball. Secondly lost balls are never lucky balls, for if they were, the previous owner would still have them. Thirdly, you should not have spare time on the golf course, unless you have snuck on to a private course, in which case you should be doing cart stunts and hill climbs. Finally, hang up your ball retriever for God's sake, there's really nothing more undignified. Carrying a ball retriever is like travelling with a plunger hanging around your neck.

One thing notable about roses are their thorns. If you have ever robbed a convenience store and jumped over a garden wall trying to make your escape, there are only two things to worry about – big dogs and rose bushes. At least dogs bark first, but roses are the silent killer. Next thing you know your baggy jeans are snagged on a Apricot Blend Grandiflora or some similar variety and they get ripped from your body. Thank God mug shots are only from the waist up.

Season:

Most roses bloom in the late spring and early summer, so you need to prune them when the plants are laden with beautiful roses. Unless you don't know a lob-wedge from a lob-ster, it's obvious when roses need pruning. There are great seasons for flowers, like around the holidays or when you want to cheer up Loyd the slow crossing guard down at the corner.

Yard Benefit:

Pruning roses actually spurs their growth, so prune often. You can use the opportunity to "shape" the rose plants to keep them more uniform and healthy. Your yard will look nice with beautiful roses, so grow some. Don't forget that roses have tremendous fragrances too. Your yard will smell better and so will you ultimately. Your friends can no longer say you stink. Finally, you can prune roses and bring them inside to your sweetheart, which beats snagging flowers from the cemetery every time. Note: Flowers from the cemetery are seasonal and not always available.

Player Benefits:

- This task is good for the mental game as it allows you to "stop and smell the roses," literally. A solid mental game is the key to success
- This task will teach you how to handle your clubs better and more precisely
- Allows swinging a golf club while doing work in the yard

Equipment Needed:

Since rose pruning requires a sharp pair of clippers, we're going to have to be creative. This task is going to require us to use two clubs at the same time. We'll use the three iron and four iron here and pinch them together to clip the roses. If you are one of those players who has traded in your low-irons for rescue clubs, then maybe you should put down this book and go watch Martha Stewart on the Oxygen channel? Do yourself a solid, get

Tip from the Pro:

Roses are often times bunched together in a "rose garden" and this can present a challenge for even the best rose pruner/golfer. Since the plants can be very close together, it makes it hard to do your best work without injury. To avoid injury to your lower extremities, it is advisable to not wear any pants when working in these conditions. Without pants you can move more freely, avoiding catching your pants on rose thorns. When your wife yells, "Look out for that nasty thorn", you can give her a knowing wink and leave it at that. Somebody get me the Roundup!

your low-irons back and step up. You'll also want to wear your golf glove for sure as the thorns on the roses can prick you. You may want to pick up a right handed glove on sale so you can wear gloves on both hands.

Handicap:

The only factor to consider before attempting this task is whether or not your spouse will notice your work as you learn how to prune roses with your clubs. You may hear things like, "Cheese and rice - will you put down your clubs and use the flipping clippers?" Don't be discouraged as it is easy for the ignorant to throw stones. This task is fine for people of all levels of play, unless you have those rare rose varieties you are growing for a contest, in which case you should not be reading this book anyway.

Detailed Instructions:

Rose pruning is simple but requires solid technique. As mentioned above, you'll use two clubs to pinch and snap off each rose. I am hesitant to use the words "pinch" and "snap" around some of my extended family, but they are words you need to hear.

To perform this action, position the clubs on each side of the rose stem you wish to cut, and with a quick snapping motion, pull them apart creating a scissor like effect. With practice the rose should cut cleanly. Resist the urge to swing the clubs back away from the stem and then slamming them together. This presents several problems, the first of which is smashing your clubs together.

You only want to smash your clubs after a poor shot or when making noise to signal for help from an overturned cart; otherwise this is bad. Also, you may not hit your target squarely and end up with a half-cut rose. These hang straight down and look horrible. Your spouse may call you something offensive if you leave roses in this condition.

There is a subtlety here that some of the best golfers should consider, and that is that the cut itself should be done on a bias or angle. Those of you with a slice know exactly what I mean as you hit the ball on a bias all the time.

Be careful with the trimmings as they can be arranged into a lovely bouquet for a loved one. Gather them up into a nice arrangement. Be sure to put these in water right away or they'll wilt.

I have heard that in some parts of the world they use two clubs like scissors to prune the roses. In this case, you lay the clubs over the stem with the stem positioned between the two club heads. At this point, you rip the clubs outwards, causing a scissor effect that nips the rose cleanly. If you attempt this move, watch your follow through as you might prick yourself.

Tree Trimming

Many of you golfers have had the wonderful experience of hitting your ball into a tree somewhere. The cliché, "Don't worry about the trees. They are eighty percent air", makes as much sense as saying, "Don't worry about cars on the freeway. They are never in one spot for very long, so they really can't hurt you."

Fiddlesticks I say. Trees have ruined more career rounds of golf than anything else, except for perhaps the trouser burps after a breakfast burrito, but that may just be me. (That's covered more in the <u>Health care for Golfer's Book</u> sold separately.)

It's ironic that trees were originally used to make golf clubs, so to avenge themselves they get in the way on the course whenever they can. It is also no coincidence that "wood" is a key part of Tiger Woods name. It is rumored that the late Earl Woods almost had his name changed to "Earl Fairway Metal", but he felt that the trees would be kinder to his son if he kept the Woods name. I would change my name to "O.B. Stake" if the out of bounds stakes on the course would be more forgiving to me.

This book is supposed to be about home landscape maintenance, so let's focus on how to take care of the potential three wood stock that is growing in your yard right now.

For you beginners, tree trimming has nothing to do with Christmas. Rather, it is the art of taking care of the trees in your yard. The goal is for the trees to lose more limbs than you do in the process. Like your golf game, trees need care and feeding, otherwise they'll wither up and die, making your yard an eyesore, and the neighbors will talk about you behind your back. That conversation may have more to do with your penchant for collecting shopping carts, but that's another story.

Please note that this task does not cover tree surgery at all, as that is best left to the experts – hockey players, and right now I am not aware of a "Gardening for Hockey Players" book.

Use this task to help you prune trees, maintain a healthy root system, and ensure your trees look their best at all times.

Season:

There's never a bad time to work on trees, but the best time is when they are small. See, trees get bigger over time and they have a habit of growing fast, especially when you are not paying attention. The Japanese have been performing the art of Bonsai for centuries and they have learned how to keep trees small. They also make very tiny chain saws to handle their bonsai trees. Sometimes they have tragic Bonsai forest fires that need to be put out with a large glass of water.

My Dad planted some pine trees on his barren lot when we moved into our new house some forty plus years ago. Neil Young had not moved to town yet. The trees were in five gallon cans and cost three dollars back in the day. Now some tree guy wants $5,000 to take them out! My Dad has decided to let the trees grow as that is a lot of cash to take down a tree he paid three bucks for. Besides, there is a small family of Ewoks living amongst the trunks.

The more you can take care of trees when they are small, the better off you'll be. Besides, chopping through a small branch on a young sapling is much easier than hacking through a six inch branch of a pine tree.

Yard Benefit:

Without trees, your yard would be a desert, and if your yard was a desert, you would be in Palm Springs, Las Vegas, or Abu Dabi. If you were in these places you would want a tree, so there you have it, your yard needs trees. Trees give your yard grandeur, color, and most importantly shade, especially if you are in Las Vegas.

Player Benefits:

- Pruning and trimming trees with golf clubs builds muscle and strength that is needed on the golf course, particularly if your ball is behind a tree and you need to hook a ball around one like Tiger does sometimes. Become friends with trees.
- Allows swinging a golf club while doing work in the yard

Equipment Needed:

This is one task that may require some tools in addition to your golf clubs. No fool would attempt this task without proper tools, which is why you'll also need a whistle and a hockey stick.

The best clubs are the low irons as they have longer shafts and can generate more club head speed. You'll need that speed for some of the deeper cuts you'll be making.

If I have not said it before, you may want to borrow a neighbor's clubs for this task. Be honest and tell him you are going to chop down some trees this weekend and he'll give you a wink and look very proud. Of course he thinks you'll be playing them on the course. Imagine his surprise when he sees you taking a full swing with his four iron at the Japanese maple that has grown too big. Hide your own clubs as he may try to grab them and join the fun. In fact, hide everything, and lock the doors as he may get violent.

Useless Knowledge: Digital Video Recorder

The Digital Video Recorder (DVR) was only invented just 10 years ago by the people at Replay TV, now owned by Panasonic. Most people incorrectly attribute the invention to Tivo. Regardless, the DVR is one of those technologies that once you have it, you cannot live without it, nor can the family. TV will never be the same. Another technology in the "can't live without" category is the nose hair trimmer - what did men do before these things came out? Uncle Ned must have some extremely long nose hair as I have seen him using it in areas no where near his nose. I'll never borrow that device from him again.

One important note about safety – frequently trees can grow up and around power lines. Before starting any work, be sure to determine if you might come in contact with any wires that may knock the power out to your home. If your home power won't be affected, swing away, as it's really no bother if you take the rest of the block off the grid. In all circumstances make sure you maintain power to your DVR, as these devices are now "mission critical" in most homes, at least in mine. Miss a recording of "What Not to Wear" and all hell breaks loose.

In any case, do not grip down on your club, keep your hands on the rubber grip only and you should be safe from just about any potential shock.

Handicap:

Again, the beauty of some of these tasks is that they are available to all skill levels. The better your stroke, the neater your work, and when dealing with some of the older oak trees, neatness counts, believe me.

Detailed Instructions:

The first thing to determine is what kind of tree you are dealing with. A tall and majestic redwood is going to require different care than a small dogwood tree. No matter what the tree type, you'll want to learn what they look like at their best. Consult books, magazines, or drive around your neighborhood and look for healthy specimens. Just don't do it at 3:00 am with the bass turned up, unless you borrowed your neighbor's car.

With the picture of a healthy tree locked in your mind, the next thing to do is to start shaping the tree to resemble your mental image. Resist the urge to make one species of tree look like another. For example, don't try to make a pine tree look like an Italian Cypress. These trans-arbor trees never fit in well with the other trees and are often seen as freaks in the garden. They do get along well with the Goth trees however.

I will tell you that in one of my earlier jobs I worked at a company that had a co-ed softball team. The league required us to have a certain number of females on the team and we met the requirement only because "Jimmy in Accounting" came back from a long vacation as "Jane". Jimmy, er Jane, could hit like a man and we won many games because of her. Things have a way of working out sometimes.

I am not sure an Italian Cypress is a tree actually, but those buggers grow huge. My brother tried to climb one on the course to see if he could retrieve his tee ball that hooked left. After determining the ball lost, he started sliding back down the tree and quickly realized that the sharp bits of the Cypress were finding their way to his man bits. He came down very slowly after that and had some itching for a day or two.

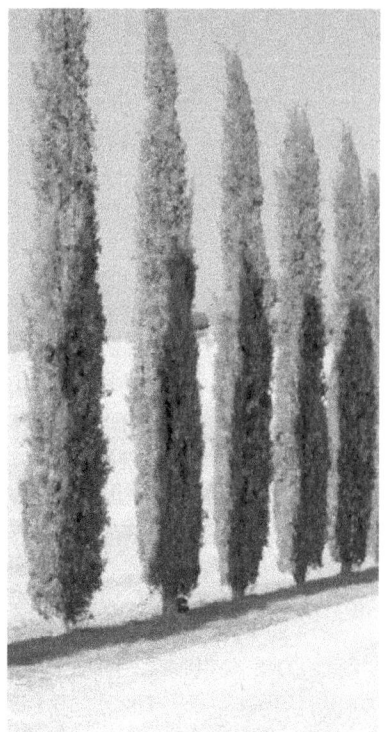

My definition of a tree proposes that if something is green colored growing in your yard and it could kill you if it fell on you, then it might as well be considered a tree. Italian Cypress meet my criteria.

Let's get down to the real details. We have not talked at all about how you get up in the tree to get started in the first place. I don't suggest taking your whole golf bag with you as it is too heavy, but one of those day bags may work perfectly. You know, the bags you take out on the local nine hole executive course where people learn to play the game. These are great places to hone your short game, and to practice tree pruning too if nobody is around. There are never any executives there by the way, so don't bother looking.

Once in the tree with your bag and a whistle around your neck, you are ready. Tree trimming and pruning always involves removing branches and other bits that should not be there. You'll know what needs to go by simply looking at it. Once you have your eye on the branch to come down, the next thing to do is to build a stance and get ready to start chopping.

The best stance in a tree is the one that keeps you from falling out of it. So find the best way to position your feet so that you are balanced

Tip from the Pro:

One of the unfortunate things that can happen when working with trees is cutting off a limb by mistake. The whistle comes in handy in this case to signal the family that a call to 911 is in order because you are injured. Better yet, if you cut a branch off a tree that you should not have, don't panic, you have some options. To hide the mistake from your wife, loosely lash that branch back in place and pray that a windstorm comes along. One time after cutting a branch my wife loved, I lashed it back in place and waited for something to blame it on. That same day a moving truck drove by and I blamed the broken branch on the truck. My wife asked how a truck going by in the front yard could clip a branch in the backyard, and I smartly mentioned that the rumble from the truck may have caused it. Sleeping with my clubs in the car that night was not so bad (except for all the trucks rumbling by) and now after 7 years the tree looks pretty good again.

and safe. Check your back swing to see if you can make a full turn at the targeted branch. Don't forget your follow-through. Make sure you have room and can turn your hips to your target. Most people that fall out of trees do so because they did not have a good follow through, or drank too many Pabst Blue Ribbons before going up there in the first place. At least the people I know anyway. If you are afraid of heights then the beer may help.

If everything looks good, start chopping at the branch slowly. Focus on a slow take away, but accelerate down until you hit the branch. For those of you who found some reason to buy one of those golf impact trainer bags, the contact with a branch (particularly a hardwood) will feel NOTHING like hitting a bag of sand. You'll know right away when you have hit the branch square as it will hurt just a little. If you are off-center at all, you may feel tremendous pain. Don't let this deter you from your work and from ultimately improving your golf game. Swing away until the branch is gone. This may take some time.

Use the whistle to call for help if you get stuck in the tree, or if due to fatigue you can no longer use your hands to get down. You can also use the whistle to call for more beer if your kids are listening. The hockey stick can be used as a tool to remove branches that may get hung up after cutting, otherwise there's no reason to have it. If attacked by birds, critters, or neighbors, you can "high-stick" them with the hockey stick.

With most trees you should start at the highest point and work down, unless the tree is greater than 100 feet tall. In that case, ask the local neighborhood teenager to assist, and challenge him to start at the top in exchange for some cash. Be sure his parents are not due home soon and he wears some kind of safety harness. The harness does not need to be tied to anything, just make sure he has it on in the event of a fall, that way you are covered by your insurance. Don't offer him beer, but be sure to tell him he does not get paid if he falls. It's these kinds of life lessons that are invaluable to kids as they grow up.

Here's the author in a tree getting ready to lose a limb. Note the stable stance, and hockey stick for clearing brush. He has a whistle too, to call for help or more beer.

Useless Knowledge: Hockey "High Sticking"

High sticking in Hockey is when a player raises his hockey stick above shoulder level and incurs a penalty. If the stick draws blood on an opponent, then the penalty is even worse. If any of this happens before or after the game, then all bets are off and players swing their sticks with reckless abandon until the cops show up. I have seen fans get into these brawls and high-stick using the tiny souvenir hockey sticks sold at the game, although these never draw blood. Support Hockey and go see a game. Buy one of those tiny sticks at the half, you may need it after the game.

If you have done your job right, you'll create a big pile of branches, trimmings, and other bits. First, pull out the pine cones, and if you have any, tee those up in the yard. They fly fairly straight if hit well, and will accentuate a hook or slice if hit improperly. Use this as a great opportunity to improve your game. The pine cones will not damage your clubs by hitting them, but watch out for kids when hitting, as kids will definitely damage your clubs.

With all the other tree trimmings left over, you are going to want to find a neighbor with a debris box in their yard. Someone always has a project going on. It's best to drop your stuff off at night so you don't disturb them.

With time and practice you'll build strength, confidence, and have some great looking trees to look at. Nice work!

Rodents, Pests, and Critters

Rodents, pests, and critters in this book refer to those living things with three or more legs (Tripeds, Quadrupeds, and so on) which you'll typically encounter in your backyard. I realize that there are people in your lives that you may consider a rodent, pest, or critter, but I doubt any of them have more than three legs. Nonetheless, some of the tips presented here may be applicable for these annoying people.

Hollywood and television have done a great job in portraying some pests in a positive light. There's Chip and Dale, the two squirrels who are so cute, but that's because you never see them gnawing through your golf bag at the turn to taste Vera Owen's delicious chicken wings on the 4th of July. Or how about Peppy Le Pew, the French Skunk from Warner Brothers? Nobody thinks that skunk stinks.

Speaking of skunks, twice I have been trapped in the garden by these cute but pesky stink bugs. The first time I was in my backyard standing on my fence looking into the neighbor's yard for firewood to borrow (he later forgave me for cutting down his prized oak tree, but I do like the smell of fresh oak in the fireplace) when a skunk came sauntering by and literally walked right past my feet. I was so scared. I am certain he wondered what that awful smell was, but at least he did not spray me. I have half-wished he did spray me as his smell would have been more tolerant than mine. That was the night before my son was born so maybe he was just giving me a break? He did not want to make a stink out of it I guess.

Useless Knowledge: Flipper the Dolphin

The Flipper the Dolphin TV series aired way back in 1964. That was so long ago that the memory in your PC right now would have cost twenty eight million dollars back in those days and the guy who wrote the first Halo video game wasn't even born yet.

The Flipper story was about two kids who lived in Key West Florida and they had a pet dolphin named Flipper. There was always some crisis and Flipper always came to the rescue. Flipper made a very distinguished sound when he "spoke". It was a great show modeled after "Lassie" (a dog), "Gentle Ben" (a bear), and the little known "Stymie" (a meerkat) television series.

The second time I had a close call with a skunk was when one wandered into my open garage while the kids and I were playing in the yard. We were stranded! We quickly jumped in the car parked in the driveway and watched and waited as the skunk explored our garage. I was nervous that my wife was going to come home and get sprayed.

In both cases I wished I had a 3-Wood in my hand, preferably a persimmon wood model of older vintage. Skunks are cute and fast, but a nice quick poke with a 3-wood will scare them off before they can foul you with their odor.

There are two rodents who are perhaps universally known worldwide. The first, Mr. Bugs Bunny, was a fantastic character who always got the best of any adversary, especially Mr. Fudd. One thing that Bugs had going for him was a superb positive attitude no matter what challenge he faced. Golfers and gardeners should take a lesson from Bugs, and remain positive no matter how many shots go out of bounds.

The second famous rodent is the chipmunk from Caddyshack. He shared many of the same traits as Bugs - positive, resourceful, and effective. He also made the same sound Flipper the Dolphin did on television, back in 1964. The Caddyshack chipmunk loved to dance and was human in so many ways - that's why we loved him. But don't be misled.

If we can de-humanize these critters then it will be easier for us to eradicate them and sleep better at night; even though we know that we are literally being eaten alive by millions of bed mites while we do.

I should be careful to state here and now that I do not believe in harming any living creature, except when it affects your golf game, then all bets are off. The corollary to this position is that since we're combining golf and gardening here, then the same holds for gardening. So, it's permissible to hurt small defenseless animals if they are going to borough under your new putting green. Let's quit rambling and get into the details about proper garden pest control and eradication.

Season:

The best season to get yard pests is the killing season. This runs from January 1st through December 31st, although Christmas is not a good day for pest control - don't be a Scrooge. There's no greater way to scar a child for life then to have him playing with his new "Jimmy the Mouse" toy on Christmas morning and then see Dad outside whipping a giant rat with a headless graphite shaft from last year's Titleist driver. This is a great exercise by the way, just be sure to have the shaft make a nice "whoosh" sound as it nears the rat.

You might consult with your local course superintendent to find out the best times to go after these pests as some of them do disappear for awhile. I am certain that the French skunks take the month of August off just like their human counterparts.

Yard Benefit:

The benefits to keeping your yard clear of rodents, pests, and critters are obvious. You won't see those telltale mounds of dirt that these critters dig up in the middle of the lawn. You'll find that these piles of dirt are quite loose and "fresh" and are actually great things to practice your sand game on. More on that later.

Player Benefits:

- Players can really hone their sand game getting rid of the mounds of dirt left behind by burrowing animals
- Allows swinging a golf club while doing work in the yard

From the Rules of Golf:

The USGA rules of golf define a Abnormal Ground Condition as follows, "An "abnormal ground condition" is any casual water, ground under repair or hole, cast or runway on the course made by a burrowing animal, a reptile or a bird." Rule 25-1 covers how to handle a abnormal ground condition and in most cases allows the golfer to take a free drop. What the rule doesn't say is whether or not any strokes taken at the animal itself count towards your score. My interpretation of that is that if you intend to hit the animal when you swing, it counts, but if you are simply taking practice swings then the shot does not count.

Equipment Needed:

Everybody has their favorite "go to" club to be used when the going gets tough on the course. You know the feeling, you shank one off the tee, reload, shank, and then top a 125 yard drive with your $600 driver. You then pull up to the ball and pull-hook your four iron eighty yards. You then take your pitching wedge and hit it fat forty yards. You then pop into the rest room, and to put it delicately, you wish you had paid more attention to what you were doing. It's at this point you need your towel again and your "go to" club.

When I get into trouble on the course and I find myself in a funk, I switch to the seven iron to keep the ball in play. This helps me get back under control and I know that with the seven iron something good will happen. Choose your "go to" club for going after game in your yard because you'll need it.

Handicap:

There's two kinds of people in this world - the hunters and the hunted. There's actually a third kind of person in this world, and that's a person who likes to divide people into groups. No matter, for this task you need to put yourself in the mind-set of the hunter. To be a hunter you need to have a plan and be clear on what you are trying to accomplish.

Before finishing that thought, there are two great soliloquies that are worth noting here - the first is Hamlet's soliloquy where his buddy Tibault was just slain. Maybe that was Romeo and Juliet, but a memorable speech nonetheless. The other great soliloquy comes from Bill Murray as the great Karl Spackler in <u>Caddyshack</u>. I quote from memory, "To catch a varmint, you gotta think like a varmint, act like a varmint, and get inside his pelt and crawl around for awhile". I'm not sure he uses iambic pentameter as his meter like the great bard Bill Shakespeare did, but the speech is powerful, moving, thought provoking, and inspirational.
If you can get yourself in Karl's mind-set, then you are ready to kill, no matter what your golf handicap.

Detailed Instructions:

Like any good hunter, the first thing to do is put up a gun rack in your pickup truck and get a duck caller. A bad trucker's hat is a nice touch if you can afford it, but those Von Dutch hats are not in vogue any more by the way. The one to get now is the cap from "Flapjack Pete's", the famous breakfast restaurants littered along the California coastal highways.

With the right setup, you can begin the process of stalking your prey. Stalking involves watching, observing, noting, studying, long periods of standing still, and a tremendous amount of patience. Don't confuse this task with preparing for the state bar exam, even though the task seems identical.

If you are going after a mole, for example, you'll want to note the location of the dirt mounds he creates and the time when he creates them. You're going to want to get him when he is happy as a clam digging away under your grass. For those of you who were not paying attention just now, I did not say there are clams under your grass.

For other pests and critters, learn what they like to eat and when they like to eat. Most of these critters are very active at night, so you may have to stay up late to gather your intelligence about their habits. Once you understand their motivation, patterns, and behavior, you are ready for the next step.

Setting the trap. To trap your prey, you need to know first what you are going after, and secondly, what you intend to do with the pest once trapped. Here is some guidance:

These guys are good! This animal can take your lunch, snacks, and cookie faster than you can run back to your cart from the tenth tee box. Guard your nuts!

Ground Squirrels:

I almost feel bad for these guys, they are not good enough to be tree squirrels so they have to live in the ground and be confused with the common mole. Second class citizens in the animal community, they are like associate members of the squirrel country club as it were. Ground squirrels can be caught with a special device that traps them, but also rams a steel spike through their head to ensure they don't get away. This usually kills them, but sometimes they get away with a nasty headache.

Skunks:

Skunks like to eat just about anything, but they prefer vegetables and raw ground turkey, just like Aunt Edna. Unlike Aunt Edna, they know when to go to the bathroom and will do so privately. The best way to trap a skunk is never, because if you do trap one, you need to figure out how to humanely remove it without getting sprayed. You may be better off to pay the kid with the slight number of teeth down the street to capture the skunk with their bare hands. If you are going to use a golf club to capture a skunk, consider using the ball retriever that extends thirty feet. As mentioned already, I have a strong dislike for the ball retriever for normal play, but in this case, and when disposing of soiled clothing on the course, it is justified in my book, and this is my book. You can write your own book about what to do with soiled clothing if you like.

Snakes:

While snakes are not pests per se, they do scare the hell out of me when I am in the garden or on the golf course. Frankly they scare me no matter where I am. Snakes do kill rodents and are pretty useful, except for the baby snakes with rattles. Snakes can be caught using special traps that get them stuck in a glue like substance, and then released to the wild or your neighbors pool cabana for giggles. Snakes should never be handled unless you are sizing one up for a nice pair of golf shoes, in which case you can approach them with your longest iron. The late Steve Irwin was quite a golfer and he used to handle snakes with a pitching wedge! That guy was insane, nobody uses a wedge with a snake. I heard he played Cobra's by the way. Did someone just groan? Steve was cool. I think everyone and every animal is going to miss that guy.

Moles:

Moles make "Carrot Top" the comedienne look handsome. Ugly, dirty, big teeth, foul, living underground, but his shows in Vegas are good, I hear. The moles can be eradicated by using one of those sound emitting spikes that drives them nuts. I am inventing a new version which pipes Carrot Top's act into the ground. That will drive the moles away for sure.

Useless Knowledge: Panther Piss

Turns out that in addition to being a fabulous deer repellent, there is actually an alcoholic cocktail called "Panther Piss". The recipe is below:

Ingredients:
2 oz Bacardi® white rum
1 oz triple sec
1 splash freshly squeezed lime juice
3 - 4 oz Sprite® soda

Directions:
Stir the rum, triple sec and lime juice together in an old-fashioned glass 3/4 filled with ice cubes. Fill with Sprite, and serve.

Never get the drink mixed up with the deer repellent, or you'll end up with some drunk deer in your yard, and your breath will be even more horrible.

Deer:

Near the higher end of the critter scale, the deer loves to eat your favorite plants and then leaves behind some cute little droppings to make you think Mr. Rabbit was in the yard, or the chocolate covered raisin rain came again. You can use panther piss as a repellent, and other products to scare away the deer, or plant nothing but Ocashia plants for them to eat. If you want to fence them out of the yard, consider a fence at least fifteen feet high.

Rabbits:

Rabbits are cute as hell and they love to eat plants, especially roses. Rabbits like to hoppity-hop around the yard, acting like everyday is Easter and you should be happy to have them there. They can stay as long as they like if they would stop eating my roses. I have seen an eagle come down and pick up a rabbit whole and have a little feast on him. If you want to get rid of rabbits, then buy some eagles to hang around and keep your roses safe. Rabbit's feet are lucky. Read more about this in the Luck chapter coming up.

No matter what the pest, there is always something that can be done to get rid of them. Please do so humanely, kindly, and with compassion as these critters are just trying to get their PGA tour card in the animal world.

Random Thoughts

Equipment plays a key role in the game of golf. Since the dawn of time man has been hitting objects with sticks to eat and reproduce, enabling survival just long enough for the next generation to develop better sticks to hit things with. The process will repeat forever.

There really wasn't any formal reason to hit spheres with sticks until golf came along. To perform many of the tasks in this book, clubs are required. Some tasks are better suited to be done with a club borrowed from a neighbor, while others require the very best that the golf industry has to offer. Hold off on any substantial golf equipment purchases until you have experienced fully some of the gardening tasks in this book. Old clubs are fine to use when getting started.

Never mix golf gloves with your typical yard gloves. Golf gloves perform poorly in the garden, and yard gloves will wear your golf grips down on the golf course. Yard gloves don't fit your hand as tightly and golf clubs can actually be thrown if not careful. I lost a club wearing some craftsman leather workmate gloves and nearly killed a wealthy patron at a private club. Her toy poodle was not so lucky, although a few stitches were all it took to get Tinker able to hold her tail high again.

Pre-shot routines are highly recommended by athletes, sports psychologists, and firing squad members, and I could not agree more. Studies have confirmed that using a routine relaxes the mind and allows the athlete to focus better, and we all know that keen eyesight is a huge advantage.

Useless Knowledge: Top Tennis Players

I am told that a study was recently performed of the top tennis players in the world and it was observed that these players all shared one trait in common - they all had routines they followed identically during matches. For example, Roger Federer might bounce the ball exactly twice before service, or John MacEnroe might have a bar fight before his match. That dude is a hot head. Tiger has a preshot putting routine he executes the same every time, and when he is putting well, he can't be beat. Learn from the professionals and get yourself some pre-shot routines for putting, chipping, and irons. Also look for MacEnroe in the bar at his next tournament. Cross your fingers for some old school bare-knuckle brawling. Bring along your tiny souvenir hockey stick just in case Gretzky shows up.

Sunscreen should be standard equipment in every golf bag. There's nothing worse than an old salty golfer who did not wear sunscreen earlier in life. Telltale signs include neck skin that looks like it was grafted from an elephant's scrotum, and facial skin with the texture of a large strawberry. Sunscreen is rated using an SPF rating. SPF stands for Sun Protection Factor, and the higher the number, the more protection you get, supposedly. I use an SPF so high that I need a flashlight to see. Sunscreen should be applied liberally, so quote Noam Chomsky or think about saving the whales while applying it.

Sunscreen is inherently greasy, so try to avoid touching your grips after a fresh application. If you have just applied some sunscreen, now is a great time to pull another player's driver out and take some practice swings. My beef with sunscreen is that no matter what the label says, it always gets in your eyes and causes burning. This can seriously affect your game and your ability to land a Boeing 747, so use sparingly above your eyes. If you do experience a burning sensation after applying sunscreen, check to see if you are urinating, and if you are, see a doctor and perhaps a lawyer immediately.

While not technically in the sunscreen family, Chap Stick® is worth mentioning here. Except in Tennessee where they have bigger issues with dental hygiene, taking care of your lips is important. Chap Stick is invaluable in bright sun locations, particularly the desert and lower Antarctica. Be careful not to put on too much chapstick, as it clumps up and can look like you might be foaming at the mouth.

Whenever I have an idle moment, I sometimes find my way out in the garden just to enjoy the surroundings and look for more things that can be improved. Like a hiker who carries a big stick, one should always have a club in his or her hand. The utility of this is immeasurable - you can use the club to poke around under bushes, flick dog and cat droppings into the neighbor's pool, and sometimes threaten Charlie, the dog who lives on the corner. This Jack Russell Terrier is smarter than most people at the bus stop, and he likes to get into our trash. There's nothing more enjoyable than a nice six iron punch shot to scare Charlie for awhile. I would not hit him mind you, but a hearty practice swing within earshot is enough to scare a dog back home to his bed.

Watering

One of the responsibilities of taking care of plants is ensuring they get enough water. Golfers have a natural instinct to avoid water, and that instinct works well in the garden too.

There's nothing worse than putting on a nice pair of light khaki golf pants and spilling water on them when tending to a dried out plant. You soon find yourself trying to explain to your family what happened and they'll laugh and point at the stain - "How did the water only wet the back of your pants in the butt-crack, Dad?" and "What does wetting your pants in the garden have to do with the mess you made in the bowling alley, Dad?". Kids have no respect for adults anymore. That incident at the bowling alley was not my fault by the way. I had some dim sum earlier and I think they put too much chili sauce on it. Sometimes you can get too relaxed, if you know what I mean. I had a blast at the bowling alley, just not the kind I intended.

In spite of the krypton-like effect that water has on golfers when playing, there's no penalty in the garden for touching water.

Plants have very simple needs - water, air, soil and sunlight. It has been proven that singing to plants, in spite of common belief, does not make them grow. Don't let this stop you from humming the Golf Central theme song in the yard. Just don't expect it to make your plants grow faster.

Since we have already mentioned Chinese food, let's explore the Ying (love) and Yang (hate) of water a little deeper (pardon the pun). One of the best science fiction books of all time is the classic <u>Dune</u> by Frank Herbert. This was also one of the worst movies of all time, directed by

Book Review: Dune

From the Dune website, "Frank Herbert's Dune series is one of the grandest epics in the annals of imaginative literature. It is science fiction's answer to "The Lord of the Rings", a brilliantly imaginative epic of high adventure, unforgettable characters, and immense scope."
In the book there is a great line that applies to fear and it may help your golf game - "I will face my fear, and I will allow it to pass over me and through me, and when it is gone only I will remain." You still have to hit your shot though.

David Lynch and starring Agent Cooper Kyle Maclachan. His sister, Sara, is a great singer by the way. The movie was a disaster partly because the book was so good and expectations were high.
All references to Dune in this chapter, with the exception of any mention of Bandon Dunes, refers to the book by Frank Herbert. Let's just forget the movie, again.

One of the central themes in Dune was preservation of water. Water was the key resource around which the world in the book revolved. People in the book wore "still suits" that recycled body moisture so the person would not go thirsty. If Craig Stadler wore a still suit he could quench the thirst of three men and a small boy. At close to five dollars per gallon for water here in the US, we're not far off from the world of Dune. Frank Herbert was on to something.

So water in the garden needs to be rationed and conserved so that it is used minimally and efficiently. Your garden watering needs to be well thought out so that you are getting optimal use of this precious resource.

Those of you who favor the giant expanse of lawn must also enjoy the giant water bill you get every month. Grass costs a fortune to water, so you need to be judicious in your use of grass. If the costs of tapping into your neighbor's sprinkler system are prohibitive, a better ground cover material for large spaces is the native weed. You don't have to water weeds and some produce nice flowers. The great thing about weeds is that there is literally no care required. Just stop watering your lawn and the weeds will show up eventually. You can mow weeds, by the way, and they look good for a day or two when freshly cut, just like your real lawn.

Water on the golf course has a well-known effect on golfers - anxiety. Anxiety leads to getting tense, and getting tense tightens muscles, and tight muscles prevent the swing from being free, which leads to a hard shank into the Ladies Auxiliary President standing by, which leads to an ambulance ride, which leads to a lawsuit, which gets you in hot water. It all starts and ends with water. All because of a tranquil lake that some golf course designer thought would be captivating.

I have seen players hit wayward tee shots when there is a drinking fountain nearby, let alone a lateral water hazard. There are some key things to know about managing water on the golf course and in the garden. Let's start with the golf course.

Many people ask, "At what point should I attempt to hit my ball out of a water hazard versus taking the penalty?"

The answer to that is very simple - "don't hit your ball in the water in the first place." The odds of shanking a ball into the Lady Auxiliary President's spleen are low, and you are better to play that shot rather than attempt to fly the lake. Seriously, I am told that if more than half of the ball is above water, then you should try to play it if you have a shot. If you are going to attempt a shot from the water, please use a camera or phone that captures video, as these shots are always spectacular. You could win yourself some money on America's Funniest Videos (AFV), which more appropriately should be called "Hilarious Videos Between Long Segments of Boring Banter or HVBLSBB". (Note to AFV Producer - We just want the videos!)

"Do water hazards have ball magnets in them because my ball always seems to get pulled into them?"

Water hazards are actually giant magnets that give off positive ions, especially if there is lots of movement with water falls or fast currents. If your ball gets attracted to these giant magnets, you may have too much iron in your diet. See our web site for a small magnet you can carry that counteracts the effects of water hazards.

We sell our very best magnet for $129 USD. Keep these away from your credit cards! In fact, keep your spouse away from your credit cards. It's safe to have your magnet and your spouse together, just not with your credit cards.

Useless Knowledge: Iron - The Mineral (not the golf club)

Iron is a mineral the body needs to make hemoglobin. Hemoglobin helps carry oxygen from your lungs to the rest of your body. A low blood iron level may be caused by not getting enough iron from food or by losing blood. If you do not have enough iron in your blood, you may get iron deficiency anemia. Iron deficiency anemia may cause problems with a child's growth and development, and cause other health problems in adults. Too much iron in your diet can cause your golf ball to be attracted to large water magnets. But there's hope - buy one of our counter-acting magnets for $129 USD.

Useless Knowledge" Skipping Rocks

Rocks are able to skip along the surface of water because of the passage of Newton's Third Law. This basically states, "For every force there is an equal and opposite reaction force". When the rock pushes down on the water surface, the water pushes back, and if the rock is spinning, it can skip along the surface until friction slows it down, or it hits your cousin in the eye.

The Guinness Book of Records lists the current record as thirty eight skips in 1994. Skipping stones is an ancient pastime. The British call it 'stone skimming'. The Irish use the term, 'stone skiffing'. The Danish call it 'smutting'. The French call it 'ricochet', and we sometimes call it "a waste of time". Quit throwing rocks and get back to golfing!

"Why are all water hazards flat?"

Most water hazards are flat because of gravity. Flat water hazards allow your skulled tee shot to skip several times off the surface and sink just before the ball would clear the hazard. If a water hazard surface is sloped, then it is time to take cover as you are most likely in a typhoon or hurricane.

It's a tradition at The Masters Golf Tournament for the players to hit skipping tee shots on hole sixteen during the practice round. The crowd loves it, and every now and then someone hits a phenomenal shot to the par three green.

Short Game Guru Dave Pelz had an article in Golf Digest that actually recommended skipping shots off the water when conditions are right. Nice tip, Dave, as that shot will come in about as handy as a urinal mint in a candy store. Maybe you can show us how to hit a tee shot off the ball washer?

"I am not sure of the proper procedure when my ball goes into a yellow staked water hazard"

This one is easy if you follow the proper steps. First, determine if anyone saw it go in the hazard. If not, then you can ask yourself the question - "What hazard?" and then play with impunity. Use the foot wedge, hand wedge, or other "special clubs" at your disposal to get your ball in the best position possible. Play from there. If someone saw it go in the hazard, then you need to determine the point at which it actually crossed the hazard. Ignore this point and drop the ball in the best position possible, and play from there. The only reason you may need to remember where the ball actually crossed the hazard is if the guy with the botched LASIK eye surgery in your foursome thinks your ball crossed somewhere worse than it actually did. You can then correct him and play it properly.

"Is it safe to drink the water in the lake?"

I can't speak for all courses, but I will say that most bodies of water at golf courses are chock-full of chemicals and other material that you would probably find in your diet cola, so have at it. Uncle Mort liked to tinkle in the water hazard at the local course; which offended some, as the hazard was a fountain in the dining courtyard. Don't ask what he did in the sand traps.

I have talked a great deal about water and the golf course. Let's turn our attention to the garden. Make sure your irrigation systems and related plumbing are tight. There's no greater waste of water than a leaky pipe. There's also nothing more embarrassing than a leaky pipe, but we'll save that for the health chapter.

One time my family came back from a weekend getaway to find that one of the sprinkler valves had blown and water had been gushing down the driveway for days. Thankfully, the water district offered a one-time special credit for just this occasion. I informed them that my neighbor might have backed his car into my pipes and was squarely to blame - he may have been responsible, who knows, as I wasn't home. I got the special credit and my neighbor lost his. That worked out. Now that is water management in the garden.

I have mentioned in another chapter about the modern garden water management practice of tapping into your neighbor's sprinkler system. This is easily done when they go on vacation; better yet, if they leave you to watch things for them, as you then have full access to their system. For example, you may not like the schedule they have set for their sprinklers and you may have to make adjustments to get things just right. If you are running a drip system, they'll hardly notice the extra water or drop in pressure.

Regardless of the source of your water, you still need to make the best use of it. On the planet of Arrakis in <u>Dune</u>, every effort was spent to conserve each precious drop of water. Do the same here on Earth. Read the book, learn from it, and skip the David Lynch movie...

Useless Knowledge: Lasik Eye Surgery

From the FDA Web Site

"LASIK stands for Laser-Assisted In Situ Keratomileusis and is a procedure that permanently changes the shape of the cornea, the clear covering of the front of the eye, using an excimer laser. A knife, called a microkeratome, is used to cut a flap in the cornea. A hinge is left at one end of this flap. The flap is folded back revealing the stroma, the middlesection of the cornea. Pulses from a computer-controlled laser vaporize a portion of the stroma and the flap is replaced. There are other techniques and many new terms related to LASIK that you may hear about."

Tiger had Lasik surgery! Many people don't realize that before the laser, this surgery was performed using a dot-matrix printer. The quality wasn't nearly as good and the dot-matrix models were very noisy.

You can't have a golf book without John Daly in it somewhere, especially when talking about nutrition. Here's John using a low-iron to chop leaves for a salad he is making. It's also cool that he is holding his caddie's cigarette for him.

A true gardening golfer...

Nutrition

Just like a golfer needs food, so does a garden. We just covered irrigation, so let's talk about food. Gardens need fertilizer and other substances for plants to survive and look great.

Golfers need food too. I am not talking about the double-cheeseburger with bacon and curly fries at the nineteenth hole. I am talking about food to eat on the course while playing. Many golfers don't realize how important their energy level is during a round of golf. Golfers complain of losing it on the back nine, and this is usually due to a drop in energy, or an increase in alcohol consumed, and sometimes it is both.

You can't have pizza delivered on the course, at least where I play, so you need to bring some food with you. The best snacks for a golfer to eat are trail mix type items, which provide energy and protein. Then Pepto-Bismol. The pink stuff is handy when the Cobb salad you ate thirty minutes ago at the turn leaves you feeling like a corn cob is making the turn in your intestines. Wow!

Plants like fertilizer. This magic stuff makes grass grow green and tall, plants sprout new growth, and fruit trees pop with fruit. To give plants food in the garden, there are a few things the gardening golfer needs to know.

There is a time and a place for everything, except spontaneity, of course. There is also a time and place for fertilizer. It's the right time to fertilize when it says so in the garden section of the newspaper, and also anytime your wife thinks the yard needs it. Hopefully the timing of these indicators is in synch.

Useless Knowledge: Fertilizers

Wikipedia (www.wikipedia.com) says that "Fertilizers are compounds given to plants with the intention of promoting growth; they are usually applied either via the soil, for uptake by plant roots, or by foliar feeding, for uptake through leaves. Fertilizers can be organic (composed of organic matter, i.e. carbon based), or inorganic (containing simple, inorganic chemicals). They can be naturally-occurring compounds such as peat or mineral deposits, or manufactured through natural processes (such as composting) or chemical processes (such as the Haber process)."

Stated more directly, fertilizers are usually made up of dung from larger animals like the cow or elephant, but never the field mouse. It's a simple matter of volume since it would take many mice to produce the same amount of "fertilizer" as a cow or Aunt Edna.

You need to use the right fertilizer for the plant you are about to fertilize. Fruit trees need "citrus" fertilizer, roses need rose fertilizer, and Italian Cypress need grated parmesan cheese. Not really, but the Italian Cypress do enjoy some red wine poured about the base of the tree. Don't use the cheap stuff; those trees can tell.

Speaking of Cypress, if any members of the Cypress Point Club in Monterey, California, would like to take me out for a round, you can reach me through my web site. Okay, I'll join if you like as an honorary member, but you have to ask before Augusta does. By the way, the Cypress Point Golf Club has just been voted the "Number One" private course in America, edging out Pine Valley in New Jersey. My odds for playing Cypress just got worse.

Applying fertilizer sometimes requires the proper tools. Lawn fertilizer, for example, requires a spreader. This tool spreads the fertilizer out evenly on the grass so that you don't burn the grass with too much fertilizer. My experience has always been to start rolling the spreader, hit something, and dump way too much fertilizer in one spot, creating what amounts to large third degree burns in the lawn. These lawn scars never go away. Dog urine has the same effect on your lawn, so never load your spreader with dog urine. Just be careful.

You can purchase one of these fertilizer spreaders from our web site for only $6,000 each. They may look exactly the same as the twenty dollar variety you'll see at a home improvement store, but ours are way better. We'll monogram them with your initials if you like. If your name is "Scotts", then your name is already on them in bright letters, as shown in the photo on the next page. We only need to sell 50 units @ $6,000 each to pay for a Cypress Point Club membership. Then I can play golf with Clint.

If you think that books like this might give some practical hints about the right fertilizers to use with your plants, you are wrong. Anyone can do that, and there already are plenty of books on the subject of proper plant fertilization, so go buy one of those. I bet you won't find any mention of

Here's the author fertilizing the lawn using fresh material from a poodle named Mikey and one of our fancy $6,000 spreaders.

This is a stunt dog, don't try this at home. Depending on the size of your lawn, you may need several pets to complete the job.

golf in those books. Don't mention fertilizing to Uncle Mort, as he has a whole different idea of what that means.

This book takes things to the next level by telling you what not to fertilize your plants with. Motor oil, cooking grease, raw sewage, and gunpowder are poor fertilizers to name a few, and here's why:

Motor Oil

If you are a person who likes to change your own oil, there's nothing more tempting than dumping out the old oil under your pine tree. Aside from the obvious environmental concerns, the real problem is that if you change your oil every three thousand miles like you are supposed to, you are going to end up with your own La Brea Tar Pit eventually, and the pine tree is going to fall over due to the oil softened soil. Look to your neighbors for help and see if you can't spread your oil out on their lawn some evening, after midnight is best. Done right (using our $6,000 spreader on setting #4 if you must) the oil is almost undetectable!

Cooking Grease

Cooking grease is not a good fertilizer either. I tried dumping out some grease we used to make taquitos along the back hedge and found this attracted flies and did not help the plants at all. The bigger problem was I always got hungry for Mexican food whenever I pruned the hedges.

Sewage

Raw sewage is an obvious "no-no." I am not talking about thousands of gallons redirected from the sewer system, but the output of one "Janga the day-laborer". He nearly ruined our rose garden by not cleaning up after what I can only politely call an uncontained personal spill. Working near the cooking grease may have set him off, but I'm not inviting him back. No more taquitos for him either.

Gunpowder

Gunpowder seems like a great fertilizer. It is powdery, dark, and loaded with potential energy. They'll look at you strangely and usually call the authorities if you try to purchase too much gunpowder at one time, but in small quantities nobody should bat an eye.

Hunter types who load their own shotguns shells often find themselves with extra amounts of gunpowder. One such fella was my Uncle Jim. What Uncle Jim used to do was take any shells or fireworks that were duds and dump them out in the back ivy. Last year an ill-fated lightning strike hit that patch of ivy, and the ensuing explosion rocked Uncle Jim's house several inches off the foundation. Aunt Annie's back was somehow fixed in the explosion though, so things worked out. In better health, she soon left Uncle Jim for a donut maker, but that's a hole 'nother story.

There are other products and chemicals that simply can't be used to fertilize plants and most of these have something to do with the periodic table I studied in eighth grade chemistry. I wish I had paid more attention at the time, but I do remember that there are some chemicals that go well together, like Pepto and Bismol, and others that don't like nitro and glycerine.

I also remember that my chemistry lab-partner Ricky Vanderkamp would come in every day and tell us how he would sneak his dad's car out at night for joy rides. I was in awe of this bold twelve year old until that morning arrived that we all knew was inevitable, Ricky came rushing in and slowly mentioned that....he saved a fortune in car insurance by switching to GEICO. Seriously, he did get busted by his dad, and I blame Ricky for distracting me from my chemistry studies.

The best thing the aspiring gardening golfer can do is research the kind of plants you have and figure out the best things to feed them. The same holds true for golfers on the course - eat something good that is going to keep you going, but don't eat any fertilizer. That's for plants. Stay away from dog urine and keep a wary eye out for "Jango the day-laborer". He may be closer than you think.

Here's the author and family in Las Vegas to attend the 2006 Tiger Jam, with Sting as the lead act. We ran into Tiger at the Nike Golf Store and Anthony was given a pin by Tiger's Mom. What a treat! Sadly, Tiger's Dad, Earl, passed away two days later.

Course/Yard Management

Most gardeners spend little time considering course management, since that would make as much sense as considering how to build the flying car in <u>Chitty-Chitty Bang Bang</u>. Course management plays a key role in the golfer's game as it does when working in the garden.

Managing the garden should be approached like managing the golf course. There's a right way to do certain things, a wrong way, and then there's the hard way. The right and wrong way are self-explanatory, while the "hard way" is a bet you make at the craps table. Not great odds on that bet by the way, but a fun bet at times, especially when it hits. If you ask to bet on a hard five at the craps table (which is impossible by the way), they'll take you out back and give you a knuckle sandwich. In this book the hard way is that path you take that usually ends unfavorably, but something is learned along the way.

Sometimes learning is the most important thing you can do, like getting the names right of your cell mates in the pokey. Or the first time you teed up a golf ball in your brother's mouth and later learned from the oral surgeon that you would have done less damage with a rescue club off that lie. I said the "first" time you teed up a ball in your brother's mouth, we only did that a couple times, for the record.

Just like you learn the hard way that feeding steak to a lion by hand at the zoo is not smart, there are many similar examples of lessons learned in golf and gardening. Feeding fruit to the lion is less dangerous by far, since they don't like watermelon and despise the cantaloupe. No matter what you try to feed the lions, they'll still try to eat your hand in the process.

Google Page Rank Explained

According to Google's website, "PageRank relies on the uniquely democratic nature of the web by using its vast link structure as an indicator of an individual page's value. In essence, Google interprets a link from page A to page B as a vote, by page A, for page B. But, Google looks at considerably more than the sheer volume of votes, or links a page receives. For example, it also analyzes the page that casts the vote. Votes cast by pages that are themselves "important" weigh more heavily and help to make other pages "important." Using these and other factors, Google provides its views on pages' relative importance."

I am sure that makes sense to somebody. If your enemy wants you to disappear, they just need to have you removed from Google and you'll never be heard from again. Powerful.

Before we look at a few cases of "hard way" lessons, let's consider why course or garden management is important in the first place.

The goal of course management in golf is to ultimately lower your score without injuring yourself or someone else nearby. The goal of yard management is to absolutely minimize time spent in the yard so you can go golfing when finished, and put into practice your golf course management skills. So one leads to the other ultimately.

Everything in the universe ultimately leads to golf, just like the "Six Degrees of Separation/Kevin Bacon" concept. (Now that I have linked Kevin Bacon into golf, this may improve this book's page ranking yet again in Google. Genius.)

The definition of the word "management" may be useful here. According to the dictionary, management means "the act or manner of managing; handling, direction, or control." It also means "the person or persons controlling and directing the affairs of a business, institution, etc." which is more in line with the traditional labor union sense, such as "Stick it to the man (management)" and "Don't let the man (management) keep you down." We're not going to get into that kind of management in this book.

Back on topic, let's figure out what acts of managing, handling, directing and controlling are important on both the golf course and in the garden. Management implies planning and execution (not the Jimmy Hoffa kind of execution) so let's do that in the garden. You need a game plan.

Since time is of the essence, the goal is to put together a plan that takes the least amount of time to execute. So where do you start? Well, you start at the beginning, of course.

The first thing to do is to make a list of all the tasks that need to be done. Don't focus on the order of things, just do a brain dump and get everything you need to do in the garden down on paper.

In the garden you can think of all the things that have been bothering you all month, like the dead blackbird on the driveway, the weeds growing in the doormat, the over-grown ivy where the rats usually vacation in the summer, and that bubbling water spot in the backyard where there might be a leak. You can use this list to plan your efforts.

What follows is a sample list of things that I might need to do in my yard. Some of these are seasonal, some are weekly, and some are to be avoided at all costs. Your list may vary depending on what you have in your yard. For example, Oprah has two lakes and pond, or two ponds and a lake on her property, so I imagine she needs to add tasks for taking care of these bodies of water. I am sure she does all the work herself, by the way.

TYPICAL GARDEN TASKS

- Mow the lawn
- Take a few practice swings with a club
- Blow off the patio with the leaf blower
- Trim the roses
- Pull any weeds
- Hit an iron off the hardpan
- Prune the trees
- Test/Fix the irrigation system
- Look for evidence of rodents or children, and clean up accordingly
- Fertilize the lawn, fruit trees, and roses
- Pick up any beer cans, confetti, or any other remnants of the last party held
- Check all drainage systems to ensure that water will always flow away from the house.
- Take a break
- Hit flop shots with foamy golf balls over the house
- Water the potted plants
- Borrow a potted plant or two from a neighbor if they are on vacation. Change the pot though or they may notice.
- Check plants for disease or insects. Look out for white flies, snails, and other mammals that can ruin your yard. Snails may not be mammals, but you get my drift.

Now take your list of things you need to do and then put them in an order that makes the most sense as I have done below:

REORDERED GARDEN TASKS

- Take a few practice swings with a club
- Hit an iron off the hardpan
- Hit flop shots with foamy golf balls over the house
- Take a break
- Mow the lawn
- Blow off the patio with the leaf blower
- Trim the roses
- Pull any weeds
- Prune the trees
- Test/Fix the irrigation system
- Look for evidence of rodents or children, and clean up accordingly
- Fertilize the lawn, fruit trees, and roses
- Pick up any beer cans, confetti, or any other remnants of the last party held
- Check all drainage systems to ensure that water will always flow away from the house.
- Water the potted plants
- Borrow a potted plant or two from a neighbor if they are on vacation. Change the pot though or they may notice.
- Check plants for disease or insects. Look out for white flies, snails, and other mammals that can ruin your yard.

As you may have noticed, it is easy for a golfer to organize the list in such a way as to focus on what is really important. But seriously, there is a reason for the order taken. Let's start at the top of the reordered list.

Taking a few practice swings with a club is a great way to loosen up before a serious session in the garden. Working the garden is like working out, and I usually work up a big sweat, so I like to start off nice and loose.

Take a few swings with two clubs at the same time to loosen up quickly. Too many swings and your wife won't respect your garden work, so be sure to strike a balance here. You may need to hide while doing this warm up.

Next, hit some irons off the hard pan. I found this warm-up great to prepare me for some of the garden tasks that require concentration, focus, and a little luck, like rose pruning or borrowing the potted plant from the vacationing neighbor. If you have ever seen Tiger hit a two iron off a concrete cart path you'll appreciate practicing this skill later, particularly if you play a lot of desert golf.

Hitting flop shots with foamy balls may require some explanation, so please forgive the slight tangent to explain. Back in the 1930's when corn was scarce, men used to...Ignore that, please. Foamy golf balls are these spectacular golf balls that are extremely spongy and they fly very true. The also don't hurt at all when struck in the "trouser weed" by a young son who thought Dad was pruning roses.

Foamies are fun to hit in the yard when you can't hit a real ball with a long iron. Some of my neighbors are golfers, although none have invited me to play at their swanky clubs, like La Cumbre Country Club in Santa Barbara, or Valley Club in Montecito. Valley Club was designed by Allistar MacKenzie by the way. The lack of invitation may stem from some of my antics described in this book, but I would think one of them would hook me up. Maybe, once this book hits the best seller's list, I'll get an invite.

Our house has a large plate glass window in the front and back so you can look right through the house and see the backyard and Pacific Ocean when there's not a fire burning somewhere. What I like to do is plop down a foamy golf ball as close to the front window as I can, and swing away with my 64 degree lob wedge to flop them over the house. The shot looks impossible. Now my son is doing it and it is starting to make my wife very nervous.

Useless Knowledge: Flight of the Conchords

I would be negligent if I did not make mention of New Zealand's fourth most popular digi-folk paradists, Flight of the Conchords. Their series of the same name on HBO is the most brilliant comedy show to appear on that channel since the Larry Sanders Show back in the nineties. The show chronicles the trials and tribulations of Jemaine and Bret, as they try to play music in New York with an inept manager named Murray. One of the best songs of the show is "Business Time", which you can see on Youtube by clicking **here**. Sorry, this is a printed book and you cannot click on anything apparently. I wish someone had told me this before I printed 5,000 copies.

The best time to do this shot is when one of the neighbors is walking by on the street so they can see it happen. It appears I am hitting a real golf ball and I am certain the neighbors are impressed with my bravado and reckless abandon for swinging so close to the window. It's a great shot to practice as it builds confidence (See the chapter on Confidence) in your flop shot. Never use a real ball for this shot unless you are at your neighbor's house, or you intend to break the window.

Another trick shot is hitting foamies at the basketball hoop with a pitching wedge from one hundred feet, but that is not on my list of regular gardening tasks. That may be covered in my "Basketball for Golfers" book if I can find time to write that. With all that warm up work it's time to take a break from gardening!

Now that we have covered the items at the top of the list, it appears to me that the rest of the list is really self explanatory. Just to quell the critics of this book who were really looking for some insightful gardening tips, I will offer some advice on these tasks.

Blowing off the patio with a leaf blower is a simple task. Don't be cheap and get the electric blower by the way. The cord always gets in the way and the electric one is simply not noisy enough. Unlike golf, where noise is unwelcome, gardening is the opposite. Noisy gardening shows your neighbors a commitment to the activity and it demonstrates hard work, just like showing up for your round four hours early. In fact, starting your leaf blower around 7:00 am on Saturdays sends a strong message to those around you that you mean business - it's business time.

Leaf blowers are extremely strong and without care you can do serious damage. Avoid using them in the house if you can. Here's a tip - you can clean your spikes with your yard blower. Just like some of the ritzy private clubs have air hoses to clean spikes, you can do the same with your yard blower. Simply fire it up and point it at your shoes. Be careful with the wind coming out of the blower as some of it travels at high velocity. At the wrong angle you can give yourself a case of "Orchitis", which has nothing at all to do with Orchid plants.

Never be afraid to point that leaf blower at a golf ball if you get a chance. At least if you miss, you can say you blew it.

Useless Knowledge : Math Fractals

According to Wikipedia, "In colloquial usage, a fractal is "a rough or fragmented geometric shape that can be subdivided in parts, each of which is (at least approximately) a reduced-size copy of the whole". [1] The term was coined by Benoît Mandelbrot in 1975 and was derived from the Latin fractus meaning "broken" or "fractured".

The Romanseco Broccoli pictured below is a great example of a natural occurring fractal.. This is no coincidence as broccoli is healthy food for the fractal's close cousin, the rectal.

What I like to do is blow all my garden debris onto my lawn where I can then mow and mulch it up with my lawn mower. Don't blow anything onto the lawn that the mower can't tackle, however. Kid's flip-flops, frisbees, and other yard items don't mulch well, but give them a try anyway. Metal objects can be sent flying as projectiles, so watch out for those.

It might be worth noting here that whenever you mix gas powered motors with spinning blades, there is a high risk of injury no matter what you are doing. Whether its a turbo-prop airplane or lawn mower, it only takes a second to stick your dingus into the blade and wonder where your extremity went, so be careful.

So, now that everything has been blown clean, it is time to mow the lawn. If it were up to me, or if this book is at all successful, I'll get one of those fancy zero-turn mowers they use at the golf course. These mowers let you zip around the yard much like a bumper car, moving forwards, backwards, and sideways at will. With a zero-turn you can bust your yard out in half the time and have a blast too; the kind of blast you intended Not a bowling alley blast, but an enjoyable one where nobody gets embarrassed. At this point I have a simple twenty two inch mulching mower that takes forever to cut my vast expanse of lawn.

My injury with a lawn mower comes not from a spinning blade, but from being in a hurry. In my lawn I cut one area much shorter than the rest to create a chipping green. (See photo in a page or two) You can't putt on it because it's not the right grass, but you can chip to it. I spread sand into it and it really has the feel of a green when hitting chip shots. Shots hit to my chipping green make just the right sound and stop nicely.

One day, I needed to lower the cut of the mower, and rather than stop the motor and adjust it as I should have per the safety instructions, I decided to keep the motor running and reach across the motor to lower the front wheels first. I will say that I was in an awkward position, because to do this, I had to hold the kill switch down to keep the motor running while reaching. The mower manufacturer probably designed the safety switch to keep people from doing exactly what I was attempting, but I am tall and the reach seemed reasonable. What a jack-ass!

As I reached, I had a sudden feeling that can be best described as the "opposite of pleasure". This pain came from my forearm as it pressed against the white hot exhaust manifold on the mower. This was a backyard Korean Barbecue, where the meat I was grilling was my own!

I may have screamed, I am not sure, but it was over in an instant and the family came running. There I was branded with "Briggs and Stratton" on my arm and the smell of burnt flesh that would make Jeffrey Dahmer salivate.

The burn was severe and it took weeks to heal, leaving me with a small scar as a reminder of that day. So the lesson really is, hire a gardener if you can, and be careful with garden tools if you can't. Gas powered spinning things are always dangerous, even when they are not running.

Mowing itself is not so tricky. Just keep going until everything is cut. If you mow your lawn regularly sometimes it makes it hard to tell what you have mowed and what you have not. I prefer to mow every two weeks so it easier to monitor progress. Who am I kidding? I prefer to mow my grass once a month. You can tell exactly what needs to be cut when you wait that long.

I start by going around the perimeter of the lawn first and then do something different each time for the inside. Sometimes I go diagonal, sometimes I keep encircling the lawn, sometimes I try fractals, but that can take forever. The whole idea is to make the grass look neat and tidy. Another section of this book deals with edging your lawn, and no matter how you do it, this is time well spent, if you are not golfing, of course.

While mowing, look for evidence of rodents and children. Aside from the obvious droppings and gnawed wood, a child's presence is easy to detect. Look for dolls, shoes, toys, cell phones, jump ropes and so which are the telltale signs of kids who were at play and decided to leave everything behind. When asked about this, kids will usually respond that they were just taking a break and they intended to keep playing with what they left in the yard. You, of course, know that a tennis racket with grass growing

Useless Knowledge: Lawn Mower Injury

It turns out that some 75,000 people a year are injured in lawn mower related accidents; 10,000 of these are children. Please keep children away from the mowers and don't let them ride on your lap. They can fall off and get severely injured. You don't want your kids to be called "Lefty" or "Skip", so please show extreme caution around these dangerous machines. For the other 65,000 adults (which I guess includes me) who have been injured, for God's sake pay attention to what you are doing. If you are going to do something stupid, leave the kids inside and make sure there's a camera rolling and a cooler with ice nearby. The ER Doctors like it better when you can bring in the body parts on ice if you can find them.

Useless Knowledge: Dukes of Hazard Filming Location

The Target World Challenge is played at the Sherwood Country Club, just North of Los Angeles. Most people don't know this, but before the area was developed it was used for the filming of <u>MASH</u>, the television series <u>Little House on the Prairie</u>, and the original <u>Dukes of Hazard</u> television show. I am not sure if Jessica Simpson, star of the new <u>Dukes of Hazard</u> movie, has ever been to Sherwood, but she did live nearby in Camarillo when she was married to that dude on TV. What was his name again?

through it was probably not just left behind, it's been there for months. These things need to be picked up and put away, otherwise Daddy's mower will chop them up and send them flying. Don't worry about chopping up rodents however. There's nothing more exciting than having a curious mole pop his head up to see what is going on just in time for daddy on his new zero-turn mower to give him a painful haircut. Ouch!

Irrigation is covered in the book elsewhere but it is worth noting that sometimes there is nothing more spectacular than what I call the "accidental fountain".

One great thing about water is that it is always under pressure, so when the opportunity presents itself, water sprays high. This is how the accidental fountain is born. Water shoots high in the air and everyone enjoys the show. The kids, spouse, and sometimes the neighbors always come running, and its your job to fix it right away.

Sometimes with a drip system, you may leave the "accidental fountain" flowing for a few weeks because you enjoy the show and little water is wasted. Other times you come home from a long weekend away to find that your accidental fountain has been running all weekend and your water bill is going to have to be paid on the installment plan.

Sometimes tapping into the neighbors irrigation system has its rewards. If they discover the unauthorized extension to one of their zones and complain to you, tell them that this is the custom in Norway and that you are Norwegian. If you do not appear to be of Norwegian decent, then you might pick an obscure country that is more appropriate. Knowing a few words of that country's chosen language is more convincing.

Drainage is a topic that cannot be emphasized enough. Just as golf courses integrate drainage into their designs, you need to do the same. One of the leading causes of damage to homes and property comes from water. Some of this damage comes from accidental fountains inside the home, but most of it comes from rainwater that seeps in under the house. This usually happens because the land around the home is not sloped

Above is the author's lame attempt at a back-yard chipping green
and also the scene of the lawn mower burn accident.
Not visible, but just over the back fence in the neighbor's yard, are
some loose rabbits that are at high risk of injury
from wayward chip shots. See Hunting for Golfers for more details.

properly. If you can read a golf green then you probably can look around your house and see how the ground is sloped.

Experts say that golf greens always slope to the water. In fact, we're told as golfers to always consider how water would run off a green. The same holds true with your house and yard. When professional landscapers talk about drainage, they talk about "evacuation" which sounds really frightening, but is a fancy term for ensuring that water gets away from the house as quickly as possible. When the doctor talks about Uncle Mort evacuating, stand clear.

If you have water under your house, then rain water is the likely culprit. Here's a test to see what is happening. Throw several golf balls underneath your house. Throw as many as you can, as far as you can. If you have brand new expensive balls, those work best for this task.

Now once you have thrown a dozen or so, put some work clothes on and crawl under the house and retrieve them. While getting the balls, take careful note of what areas have the most moisture, so you can tell where to focus your efforts outside.

Why throw the balls? Without the balls under there you would have no reason to crawl around in a dark, moist place with spiders and other things lurking. This is a bit of a deception of course, not unlike what happened once at Tiger's Target World Challenge at Sherwood Country Club.

A spectator accidently dropped a quarter into a porta-potty. He borrowed a brand new golf ball from a friend and surprisingly dropped it in the same potty. He then proceeded to reach into the bottom of the particularly sweet potty and retrieve both the quarter and the golf ball. When asked why he did this, he said that he wouldn't reach in there just for a quarter! Now I know why Mom and Dad always cautioned against putting money in our mouths!

Weather

My goal was to have my golf score break eighty a few years ago, and this is how I did it. Young Jeff Scott and I had a conference in Las Vegas, and we bombed in Jeff's car from Santa Barbara to Las Vegas in record time. We drove straight to a course called "Silverstone" on the outskirts of town. We knew we were in for a special day when there was a tournament finishing up which featured female Las Vegas dancers as escorts for each of the foursomes. I should have said earlier that the course was on the "no skirts" of town if you catch my drift.

We teed off and played really well, thirty six holes in fact. Lo and behold I shot a seventy nine in the first round and was absolutely thrilled! This is where the weather comes in. It was so flipping hot there, above 107 I believe, and two things happened. First, every shot hit seemed to go an extra ten percent farther than normal due to the warmer air; this may have helped my score. Secondly, I did not realize it but my sinuses were drying out due to the warm air and lack of moisture. Later, at the Bellagio Hotel, I started to notice a runny nose which soon turned into a full blown sinus infection; the first I had ever had. These are incredibly painful and surprisingly debilitating. I should have paid more attention to the weather, and tried to get there earlier for the Vegas dancers.

If you are outside golfing or gardening you are going to deal with the weather. The weather will always win, no matter how hard you try to ignore it. There are some people here in Santa Barbara who wear shorts everyday of the year, and most days it is not a problem. These style masters know that there are only going to be five or six days a year when

Typhoons are created when moist air rises and the water vapor condenses, causing intense rain and thunderstorms. These storms are prevalent in regions like Southeast Asia.

The picture shown to the left is not a typhoon, but rather a picture of the ghost of Pac Man. He officially died when Halo 3 came out.

their shorts are inappropriate, and so they just endure it. There are some others here who insist on wearing only green pajamas, but that's just the folks I see around "Surgery" at the hospital.

In spite of our modern technology, we still can't control the weather, at least not to any significant degree. (Pardon the pun.) What technology does allow us to do is better forecast and monitor the weather as it approaches. There are some great weather satellite web sites, like "www.weather.com", that can show in almost real time the movement of weather fronts and the amount of rain that is expected. This is great information for taking care of your garden and managing your golf schedule.

I will tell you right now that one of my pet peeves is when some guy has his sprinklers on when it is raining. What a waste of water! This is particularly embarrassing if it is your neighbor, and you have tied into his sprinkler system, because that means your sprinklers are on too. When the clouds clear, encourage him to put in one of those fancy shut-off valves that shuts everything down when it rains. You could even offer to buy him one, as this will save you both some embarrassment when the next storm hits.

At it's essence, weather is all about changes to humidity levels. Obviously, when it rains there is plenty of moisture around, and when it heats up, things dry up. If you are in Singapore, or parts of Southeast Asia, you can have all of this happening within a ten minute period.

Through the process of evolution and adaptation, plants have learned to thrive in environments with different types of weather. So your real concern is changes to the weather that are outside the norm; this is where plants and golfers suffer. You must consider the weather when taking care of your garden. When temperatures drop, some plants can't handle the cold, and they certainly can't go live in Boca for the winter. Cover these plants and protect them from the elements. Hot sun is not good for some plant species either. I do not recommend sunscreen for plants, as it just makes them greasy. Uncle Mort liked to rub mayonnaise on our artichoke plants when we were kids, and he told us that it made the plants feel better. We could never tell, because he always ate them right after adding the mayo. Uncle Mort liked to eat things in the yard, and he was fearless about it. One time he ate what he thought was a pine cone, only to discover that one of the cats had left a hair ball behind. Good thing there was some Roundup nearby for him to wash it down with.

The most important weather condition to consider as a golfer is lightning. Golf tends to provide the perfectly wrong behavior when lightning is imminent. Swinging metal clubs high in the air is asking for trouble, so don't do it. Take shelter and let some one else "take charge" if you know what I mean.

Useless Knowledge: Struck by Lightning

According to the National Weather Service, the odds of being struck by lightning are 1 in 3,000. Of those struck, 10% are killed. This means that the odds are 1 in 300 of being killed by lightning. 84% of those struck are men, so now your odds are 1 in 252 if you are male. Lightning strike statistics on the web don't agree, so let's assume they are half right. If this is true, then now your odds are 1 in 126 of getting hit and dying. Very somber indeed.

Here are some tips for avoiding injury.

1. Stay as low to the ground as you can, but don't lay down.
2. Maintain the same stance a baseball catcher would, as this minimizes ground contact. You don't need a cup however.
3. Stay away from tall isolated objects like trees, towers, and so on.
4. Don't move until thirty minutes after the last thunder is heard. Check with Uncle Mort for false alarms however.

Tempo

George and Ira Gershwin wrote "I've Got Rhythm" and Steve Martin sang, "I've got ryth-rthy-ry-th-th-m-mmm". This could not sum up better the main affliction that hinders the musician and the golfer alike - Tempo!

It's all about tempo, that magic internal clock that tells the body and mind what to do at just the right time. When swinging a golf club or a shovel, everything needs to be in synch or you'll dig a big hole behind your ball, or make a nice gash in your ankle, or both. Although one could argue that tempo has no place in the garden, I must protest by providing several paragraphs to the contrary.

All living things have their own tempo and rhythm. Humans, as a race, like to sleep at night and sleep during the day too if they could, while other species are nocturnal, like the worm for instance. That's why they call worms "Night Crawlers", I think. Anyway, plants have a tempo or rhythm as well.

Plants are primarily in synch with the rhythm of the Sun, since that is where most get their nutrients and perform photo-synthesis, the conversion of light into wallet-size pictures. Seriously, plants, and the garden in general, grow and live to the beat of the Sun and the weather caused by the Sun. Plants are also in tune with the rhythm of the seasons, like Christmas, back to school, and Nordtsrom's Half Yearly Sale. I may be getting confused with shopping seasons, but you get my point.

As a gardening golfer it is important to understand this to be able to take the best care of your garden. So from a practical sense, how can one use rhythm and tempo in the garden? I'll tell you exactly how.

Get yourself an iPod (or similar device that is not as cool) and load it up with your best songs. (You know, the ones you like to dance to.) Now when you go out into the garden to work, crank up that iPod so that you are entertained and the time passes quickly. The plants may sense your enjoyment of the great outdoors and the music, and respond by moving just a little bit, although that could just be the wind.

Not to be selfish, consider the plants and their rhythm too. Just like Grandpa Jack doesn't like to be woken up in the middle of the night unless there's something naughty with midgets on cable, plants don't want to be watered or bothered at night either. Don't mow the lawn at night; both the neighbors and the lawn hate that. If you live in a desert community like Las Vegas or Palm Springs, it is usually cooler at night, so go ahead and mow if you must.

Beyond the daily rhythm of the garden, there's the seasonal clock to consider. Plants have a natural sense of the seasons and adjust themselves accordingly. You need to tailor the attention you pay to the garden in response.

If plants could talk, they would probably say, "Please, Master, play more golf in the summer, because I don't need much attention. It's too flipping hot to grow, so go ahead and enjoy yourself." Summer is basically the plant's way of encouraging you to golf. The other seasons are interesting, of course, but the plants need more attention at these times.

What about a golfer's tempo? Most of the great golfers I know, including my golf teacher, a good friend, and an old neighbor, are all excellent musicians. One is an expert banjo player. In some places, if you hear someone playing the banjo, it usually means that there is fresh corn being served in a mobile home park. This varies by regions of the country, of course. If there was a scale that displayed the attractiveness of musical instruments across its range, the banjo and bagpipes would be on the lower end of the scale. Still, you have to respect anyone that has mastered an instrument, and apparently their golf game too.

The fact that all these great golfers are musicians is no coincidence, I believe. Timing and tempo are everything.

These players all have the ability to execute their swing without all the shameful, poor coordination that you see at the driving range regularly, at least when I am there. These musical golfers swing with Grace and Composure, and two other girls from the LPGA, and it's all captured on video. There are no midgets on that tape, so don't wake Grandpa Jack.

Sadly, natural rhythm is not something you can buy or learn from a book. So do the best you can by turning on your iPod, start tapping your feet, and take care of the garden when your plants need it most. As the Beastie Boys shout, "Shake your rumpah!"

Looks really safe to me, he's got two 2 x 4's holding that thing up after all. He must be installing some anti-lock brakes to make that truck even safer to drive.

Safety

There's "safety in numbers" they say, but I just don't see it on the golf course. Whenever I have a high score, I don't feel safe at all. I get nervous, tense, and agitated, and once I am in that state, I am dangerous.

I was working in the garage installing some Cat five wiring and was drilling some holes for a wiring rack I was mounting. (If you read that last sentence too quickly you might think I was drilling a cat, so please read carefully.) While drilling, the drill slipped off the surface and hit my left hand, on the back left side below my pinky finger. My instincts told me the injury was significant, but before inspecting the damage like a normal person would, I immediately put both hands in my golf grip position to see if the injury was going to effect my swing. It's moments like this when you realize you might be slightly obsessed with playing golf.

Once relieved that my swing was unaffected, I surveyed the damage more carefully. Turns out the grip was fine and a few stitches took care of the injury. I played well the next day because the injury kept me from fanning open my club on the takeaway. Please don't imitate this injury to fix a similar swing problem you might have. I don't want my injury to become like the "Tommy John Elbow Surgery" all the baseball pitchers get. (See next page for more details on Tommy John.)

This section is not intended to make fun of safety in the garden or the golf course, but rather to offer some insight that can make one safer as they garden and golf.

Looks obscene, but it's really just Phil getting upset that he missed his chip at Doral in 2006. This may be where the wrist injury started...

Safety is a word and concept worthy of some discussion, because in some ways it is a misnomer. To be completely safe, one would have to live his or her life in some special, isolated environment protected from everything, and not actually move, as that may cause injury. To be safe in the purest form of the word is impossible.

Safety is more about risk and the avoidance of injury. By employing safe practices, one can substantially decrease the risk of injury dramatically. The risk is still there, but much smaller. Conversely, by ignoring safe practices, one can dramatically increase the risk of injury by doing something stupid, like trying to push a freight train over as it speeds by. You can't do it by the way. I tried and was spun so fast I broke my hip.

Most activities present a risk/reward scenario where the increase in risk can provide a very high reward. So the concept here is to mitigate risk while maximizing reward. This is important to recognize and remember as we work through this section.

So what does this have to do with gardening and golfing? Well, the obvious goal is to minimize the risk of injury while maximizing the reward from the activity. The best thing we can do is to dig into some real world examples:

Using Electric Yard Tools in the Rain

That flipping hedge in the back that grows like a weed always needs a trimming. You can't skip it because done right, it looks like a perfect green box, but left unchecked, it grows like ear beard at the old folks home. If you are going to work with electricity and water together, the risk is quite simple to understand - death by electrocution if the extension cord touches water and you are not using a GFCI outlet.

The reward can be quite high though - let's say it's Saturday and raining and you know Sunday is going to be clear as a bell. Like most golfers, you

Useless Knowledge: Tommy John Surgery

"Since the invention of the breaking ball, there has been no more significant development in baseball than Tommy John surgery."
--Will Carroll, Saving the Pitcher

Turns out that roughly 10% of the pitchers who have appeared in the majors have had the Tommy John Elbow Surgery. This procedure saved the careers of many players, who would have otherwise been sent off to the glue factory. What many people don't talk about is Tommy John's other surgery - the addition of a third prosthetic testicle. Tommy was quoted as saying, "With three balls down, I can focus on getting the ball over the plate and avoid pitching the fourth ball. I hate walking batters". You gotta love his commitment to the sport. Another up and coming surgery is the "Tommy Lee" procedure, but that won't be described here.

Useless Knowledge: GFCI Outlet

The GFCI outlet, invented in 1972, is a miracle safety product. This device senses changes in current flow and within 1/40 of a second, shuts off the circuit to prevent electrocution. Thousands of lives have been saved by this fabulous invention. This device saved Uncle Mort countless times as he liked to take his AC powered massager into the hot tub after a few pops. Whether you have a GFCI protected outlet or not, always be careful around electricity and never let Uncle Mort use your bathtub.

want to get the gardening out of the way, rain or shine, so that you can golf when the weather is ideal. So the goal is to minimize the risk or the injury, so that you can still play on Sunday.

How do we mitigate this risk? Simple really. Use an umbrella, here's how. Buy yourself a homeowner's umbrella policy to cover you in case someone gets seriously injured on your property. Next, pay the kid down the street to do the hedge trimming for you now that you have the umbrella in place. Enjoy a warm cup of tea inside while "Corky" trims the hedge. If you notice any unusual flickers of the power while he is working, be a sport and call 911 right away as every minute counts.

Climbing too high on a ladder

There's no greater reward than climbing high on a ladder and enjoying the view, especially when the young newlyweds next door are having a special pool party. We all understand the reward. The risk is falling off the ladder and breaking your neck. Sometimes you need to climb high to prune a tree or a branch, so you step up onto that top step, the one your parents told you to never stand on. Worse, maybe the ladder is still not quite tall enough so you need to really stretch to cut a branch. Dangerous! So how do we mitigate the risk of falling?

Take a step back for a moment (not literally) and understand that the fall never kills you, it's the impact. So what you really want to do is make the impact as soft as possible. Done right, you can climb and fall from as high as you like; carefree, in fact. Parachutes don't work since you are not high enough. Bungee cords might work, but there is that annoying recoil action that can hurt the neck. The best plan is to locate and prepare your landing area to ensure a smooth landing.

One product that has become quite popular is the air bed. These modern conveniences have a little motor you plug in and within seconds you have a comfy bed. If you are lucky enough to own one of these, inflate it and place it under your ladder. If you don't have one, you can buy refurbished ones from our web site for $800 each with a ten day guarantee. If you fall, the bed will slow you down quite a bit, and injury will be minimized. You are not completely out of danger yet, though, as you may bounce back in the air and land on something hard. Do not let the kids see you do this or they'll be taking dives off the ladder when you go to work. The best way to prevent that is to take the air out of the bed before you leave. That way, only the first kid will take the jump and the others will learn from his mistake. Tell your kids that it is most polite to let their guests always go first. You could take down the ladder, but that just means more work when you get home.

Safety at the Driving Range

It has been a long standing tradition of golfers on the driving range to take pot shots at the guy in the ball pickup tractor The guys driving the tractors expect people to fire shots at them, so they are ready, but this diminishes the fun. Driving range tractor drivers know only the beginners aim at them deliberately, as the better golfers are more focused on their game. The drivers worst nightmares are when the good golfers take aim at them, as the chances are very good they'll be struck.

At one course in the San Francisco Bay Area, the tractor had a target sign painted on the side - the guy was asking for it. While the reward of severely and literally rattling his cage is high, the risk for damage is high too. There's nothing worse than breaking the pickup tractor with a poorly aimed shot, because if the machine is broken, they can't pickup balls, and then you can't practice. There are lots of guys standing in line to operate the tractor, but only one tractor. High risk indeed.

As before, the best approach here is to get creative and minimize the risk and maximize the reward. If you are hellbent on hitting the tractor boy, one method some of us in the club employ is to wait until he is off duty and fire low stinger shots at him in the parking lot while he runs for his car. Remember, you are always responsible for your wayward shots, so hit the best shots you can. I have found the added pressure improves my game overall, and minimizes property damage. Don't park your car anywhere near his.

Speeding at high speed

The heading may be redundant but one is a verb and the other is a noun. Speeding in your car is a classic risk/reward situation. The faster you go, the sooner you get where you are going, and the sooner you can get back, to then speed over to the golf course. There are two risks here - First, safety related, and secondly, the risk of getting a speeding ticket.

If you study traffic accidents related to speeding, it's clear that the severity of injury increases as the speed increases, but only up to a point. Traffic accident data shows that there are very few injuries or accidents at speed in excess of 140 miles per hour. Based on this data, my theory is that the faster you go, the less likely you'll be injured. If modern cars could go 400 miles per hour, there would be literally zero accidents, assuming I have done my analysis correctly.

So, if you are going to speed, go as fast as you possibly can. If all goes well, you will lower your risk of injury dramatically. If you can't exceed 140 miles per hour, however, please obey the speed limit or you will get hurt. There are only a few vehicles that can go a sustained 140 miles per hour, the Ferrari 430 Scuderia, the Maserati MC12, the Porsche 911 GT3 RS, and the Rental Car, usually a Taurus or some other mid-size model.

Rental cars are cheaper than these other exotic cars, and they perform just as well in just about any road condition. You can hill climb, race, jump, and skid the rental car without a hitch. No need to worry about door dings at the mall either. Those expensive cars are just too delicate to use in the many situations where the rental car is so versatile. With the rental car, always decline the insurance coverage and be sure to bring the car back with a full tank of gas. If you lose any parts along the way, bring those back too.

I have not discussed the risk of getting a traffic ticket for speeding. I am in no way advocating breaking the law when the police or kids are around. On the wide open highway, what's the harm in blowing out the fuel injection system a little? Well, for starters you could break a hip if you crash. Note that at high speeds the local gendarmerie may insist on hauling you in for reckless driving, so be respectful. To absolutely minimize the risk of a ticket, be sure to carry a copy of your brother's expired license he threw out. Present that license when requested. In addition to the speeding ticket, you'll probably get a ticket for driving with an expired license, but your brother can straighten all that out when he renews his license in five or six years. You may have to intercept his mail for a little while until things calm down.

Drinking Yard Chemicals

There are some odd-balls out there who are willing to drink anything as long as it is liquid and there's the potential to adjust their attitude. Let me be perfectly clear, there is <u>never</u> a reason to drink yard chemicals. The reward is low and the risk is extremely high. Don't do it. (Roundup has a horrible after taste, by the way and it left my throat dry and scratchy. My spleen has been bothering me too, but that may have more to do with an injury suffered during the ladder fall described earlier.)

Yard chemicals should be kept in a place where kids and pets can't find them, play with them, or eat them. If you accomplish nothing else in your yard but protecting your kids from harmful chemicals, you should be able to stop at that and go golfing. I tried this argument to get out of doing some yard work, but my wife did not buy it. While she applauded my efforts to protect the kids, she sent me straight out in the rain to prune the box hedge with the electric pruner. It's a good thing she bumped my life insurance up to five million dollars when we were getting the umbrella policy. Not sure why she insisted I work barefoot, but she has grown quite fond of the pool guy. This strikes me odd as we don't have a pool.

Useless Knowledge: Skull and Bones Society

The Order of the Skull and Bones, based at Yale University, has nothing to do with labeling hazardous chemicals. Rather, this secret society is composed of Seniors at Yale who meet twice a week to tell secrets to each other. Members are called "Bonesmen" and include notable members such as George W. Bush and his father George H.W. Bush. Interestingly, Prescott Bush, H.W.'s father, was married to Dorothy Walker, who's father was George Herbert Walker. George Herbert Walker is who golf's "Walker Cup" is named after. He played a prominent role in the formation of the USGA, where all our golf rules come from. This fact makes all golfers "Associate Bonesmen" by the way, so feel free to show up at the next Skull and Bones meeting and introduce yourself.

There are so many chemicals for the yard that it is impossible to keep track of which ones are dangerous and which ones aren't. For safety sake, consider them all dangerous! Usually the ones with the Skull and Bones symbols on them indicate that these compounds are not rum from Pirates of the Caribbean (Another Google Page Rank hit there I hope), but instead something harmful indeed. Please don't drink yard chemicals, they are poison. If you are curious, you can take a small sip, but leave it at that.

Noise

While one might not normally consider noise a safety concern, it really is. We're all too familiar by now with the issues of noise on the golf course and the havoc it plays on the professional tour players.

What is so absurd about quiet on the golf course is that the quiet environment tends to amplify even the faintest sounds. The more silent it gets the louder the slightest sounds become. Someone in the gallery has their stomach rumble near the tee, and everyone looks at the guy like he just fired a gun.

I was at the Tiger Woods Target World Challenge at Sherwood Country Club and they had to have tournament volunteers manage the out house doors when there was a group on the green. The doors on the out house made a loud "whap" sound when they closed and this disturbed the competitors. The volunteers had no control over other sounds that emanated from inside the potties, however. The volunteers didn't seem to care that the dude was in the portable loo because of a violent digestion problem caused by a concessionaire not washing his hands properly, but that's a story for the Board of Health. Besides, what fun is volunteering at a world-class tournament and getting thunder mug duty? Your only hope would be that some famous player takes ill and runs directly to your bank of potties. There's no way to get an autograph in that situation, and I am not sure you would want one. A "high-five" is out of the question.

In other sports like baseball or football, there are thousands of people screaming, so one additional noisemaker really has no impact. I bet players in other sports would freak out if the fans were deathly quiet. This might be a great trick to try on the opponent, rather than hitting together those stupid inflatable plastic noise sticks.

In the garden, noise can be a huge issue. With gas-powered devices it can get very loud. This brings up a theory I have which is that the louder something is, the more work it is doing. If you have a really loud yard blower, you know you are getting a lot done. So the reward for noise is to get lots of work done, and the risk is damaging your eardrums or disturbing the neighbors. Let's discuss both along with some mitigation strategies.

As far as ear injury is concerned, you always want to protect your ears. Even if your hearing is almost gone from listening to over-amplified Police albums years ago, you never want to make matters worse. The best solution is to get yourself a decent set of ear muffs. Not the kind you wear when ice skating in Minneapolis, but some good ones made from hard plastic like the ramp guys wear at the airport. Wear these whenever you work in the yard. I have noticed that neighbors are less likely to bother me when I am wearing ear-protection, but it might also have something to do with the taser I carry, and the fact that I don't have a shirt on.

Now that you have your ears protected, let's discuss the neighbors for a moment. The big question really is, "What time in the morning is it acceptable to begin using loud power tools in the yard?" Ignoring local ordinances for the moment, or forever in my case, it's all about mitigating risk, so eliminate the problem entirely.

The best way to do that is to buy your neighbors each a set of the plastic ear-muffs and tell them you are starting at 6:00 AM next Sunday. If they complain, mention the gifted ear-muffs gracefully and suggest that

Here's the author raking golf balls in the garden.
My Dad once said that the best two balls he hit all day on the course were when he stepped on a rake in the sand trap.

perhaps their gardener could do some work in your yard during the week to prevent the weekend noise. What a great way to shut them up, get them to pay for all your gardening, and achieve the silence and inner peace we're all looking for.

Fire Safety

As I am putting the finishing touches on this book, California is engulfed in fires all over Southern California. These fires are primarily due to the Santa Ana winds, which blow so hard it is difficult to stay standing. You have probably heard of a two club wind, three-club wind, and so on when determining the effect of the wind on your golf shot. Santa Ana winds are an eight club wind at least, if you can even balance to hit your shot. Don't play with fire, around fire, or fire anyone. Keep the kids away from it too, it is just so dangerous and destructive. Uncle Mort used to say to us kids, "Don't play with Mitches", so I stayed away from any kids named Mitch or Mitchell. He said they were dangerous. As I grew older I learned Uncle Mort could not pronounce certain vowels so well, especially after a few cocktails. Now his phrase, "Don't play with fur, you will get burned" makes more sense to me.

At the very least, I hope these safety tips have given you some ideas to ensure that you and your family stay as safe as possible. From a selfish perspective, I want you to be as safe as possible, as this minimizes any potential injury to me or my loved ones. If everyone lives by this simple principle, we should all be safer. The last thing I need is you speeding at only one hundred and twenty miles and hour and crashing into my family as we're getting a shake at In and Out Burger. You should never go that fast in the drive through lane anyway. Be safe and sane, not just with fireworks, but with everything.

Not only do these guys have some pimp apparel, including Kangol berets and black boots, they got game too! That's Fidel Castro and Che Guevara playing a little golf back in the day.

Apparel & Endorsements

Where would you be without apparel? Well, you would most likely be sitting with a towel on your privates in the county jail calling for a bail bondsman. (See next page sidebar for bail bondsman tips) Even if you are not, you need apparel whether you are in jail, the garden, or the golf course.

Apparel has served a purpose for thousands of years, maybe millions. Before there was apparel, there was clothing. Clothing is defined as "a covering", much like the towel mentioned above or some old squirrel skin used by a caveman to cover himself. Apparel is defined as a decorative clothing, which would be like having a nice Ralph Lauren Polo fluffy striped towel for cover in jail, or a silky mink-skin covering the loins in the cave. I hope you see the difference. This chapter talks about apparel, not clothing.

Before we get into the stylistic details of apparel it is important to touch upon the second most important aspect of apparel behind style, and that is price. (Fit is important too, but let's trust that you'll buy the "right" size. When I say right size, I mean the actual size you should be wearing. Just because in high school you wore pants with a thirty inch waist does not mean that is the right size now that you are forty and you are now wider than taller.)

As Uncle Mort has always said, "The best price for a garment is free.", but that attitude led to a series of shoplifting arrests. He's no relation to Wynona Ryder, by the way, but he really enjoyed her in BeetleJuice. Let's take Uncle Mort's words and not his actions to heart; free apparel is the best, we agree, but the best way to get free apparel is to get an endorsement agreement.

Legal Advice

With regards to Bail Bondsman, don't ever go with the ones named 'AAA', they are just looking to be the first one you see in the phone book. Go with one that has a regal sound, like 'Coventry Bail Bonds'. Better yet, find one with someone who speaks with a British accent, as they have a way of making any act sound acceptable and expected. "Pardon me sir, but my client had the unfortunate accident of finding himself without his pantaloons while looking in his boot for a brandy snifter". Most judges will at least be impressed, if not dismiss all charges. Most judges enjoy a brandy after dinner so you might curry good favor. Never make fun of the Judge's robe however.

Endorsement agreements are established with people so that the person (now perhaps a spokesperson) will wear the company's product in exchange for cash. All the apparel is free! You want to get an endorsement agreement so you can get paid, or at a minimum get free stuff.

Just to take a slight tangent here, if I might, I have come to realize that in America at least, and in some other countries perhaps, the general population has it wrong. We buy shirts, hats, equipment and other items that prominently display the logo or brand of the manufacturer without any "endorsement" from the manufacturer whatsoever. In fact, we pay a premium for these items.

I want to break this consumer behavior by simply asking the clerk in the store to remove the logo when purchasing anything with a logo. The dialog might go something like this:

Clerk: May I help you?

Customer: I would like to buy this hat.

Clerk: No problem. That will be $42.23 with tax.

Customer: That's cool but I would like to have this logo removed from the hat first.

Clerk: Dude! Why buy that hat if you don't want the logo on it? That's what makes it cool.

Customer: I am not interested in cool (obviously), but I like the construction and materials of this hat - can you please remove the logo?

Clerk: I can take the logo off, but that might ruin the hat.

Customer: Well since you will damage the hat, can you sell it to me at a discount then?

Clerk: I can take forty percent off.

Customer: Tell you what, I'll take the forty percent discount and do you a favor and just take the logo off myself when I get home?

Clerk: Thanks man, that's cool. You just saved me a bunch of work.

Everyone is a winner, and now you have in essence received an endorsement to wear the hat. This works for any kind of garment, but tread lightly if the Store Manager is around. Look for stores with high school kids working in the afternoon.

We all know there are many endorsements in golf. Tiger makes most of his money off the course, and he clearly has aligned himself with some marquis brands - Nike, Buick, Tag Huer, American Express, Accenture and FlapJack Pete's in Southern California, but that is more of a favor to Pete. Other players have other contracts and we all know the brand names by now - Callaway, Titleist, Ben Hogan, Cleveland, Bridgestone, and so on. But what are the marquis brands in the gardening world?

Some of the gardening brands that come to mind are...well...er....there's that fertilizer company and I think Scotts makes grass seeds, and so on. Not a lot of brand recognition there, at least not with golfers anyway. We can change that.

Can you imagine wearing a "Roundup" shirt or hat? It could say, "Kill your weed with lots of speed", or something. Or what about a shirt with a big "Toro" logo on it? How about a hat that said, "Goodall Panther Piss" on it? Would you ever wear that?

A simple rule - If it's free, then of course you would, and Uncle Mort would too. Panther piss is sold by some of the finer establishments and it is used to keep deer out of the yard. Not sure it works, but I know it tastes horrible. Uncle Mort took a swig one time when he thought it was a beer. He threw up, and to this day I have never seen a deer go near him, so at least it works. He gets funny looks from animals at the zoo, however.

Go get yourself some free "schwag" to wear from some of these companies when you are golfing, gardening, or looking for a panther to capture your own deer repellent. (Just a tip - be sure to go after that panther after he has eaten and don't be surprised if he gives you a funny look when trying to collect your specimen. Others may look at you oddly too. No matter how many beers you have had, relieving yourself in the garden does not keep deer away.)

Golf and gardening both share the wonderful trait of requiring apparel that is both functional and snappy looking. This is true for golf, certainly, and maybe it is a stretch for gardening, but I am on a roll so let me continue. In both activities one needs to be covered head to toe in apparel. Let's work from the ground up:

Shoes

These are the literal foundation for the rest of your ensemble. No matter what the endeavor, comfortable and safe shoes are a must. If you can get ones with style and class, then all the better. Shoes always played a prominent role in our home growing up as kids, since one of my Dad's favorite half-serious threats when we misbehaved was that he was going to "plant his 9 1/2D Florscheim right up our keasters". He never did, but I am sure that it would hurt, and knowing my brother's hygiene habits, dad would undoubtedly have to re-shine his shoes after. Nowadays, we would just call Child Protective Services and have Dad hauled away. Times have changed.

When golfing or gardening it is really important to keep your feet dry. It's amazing how the comfort of your feet can affect your entire mood, so get good shoes that stay dry. Safety is a concern too, so never wear flip-flops when chopping bamboo with a machete unless you have more than ten toes to start with. If you have more than ten toes you should not be wearing flip-flops, no matter what you are doing.

Finally, get some shoes that look decent. There's nothing worse than a well dressed person sporting shoes that look like they came with some free cheese from the government. Don't skimp on shoes; you'll regret it. That government cheese is not bad, by the way. Keep your shoes and your cheese "sharp".

Don't go "Imelda Marcos" on shoes though. It is imperative that garden shoes or golf shoes never be worn in the house. Take them off when you come inside, otherwise, you'll track dirt, bugs, debris and perhaps some panther piss in the house. Keep the outside "outside" and the inside "inside". Besides, golf shoes in particular offer no additional grip on some of the modern linoleum used today.

One key difference between golf and garden shoes (and basketball shoes for that matter) is that garden shoes should be "high tops" or higher on the sides. This prevents dirt and debris from getting down inside your shoes. You never see high top golf shoes. You don't see high heeled golf shoes either, because they would not be practical and the ladies on the LPGA would not wear them. I may consider marketing a line of high top golf shoes for men - I envision something black with a zipper up the inside.

Socks

If shoes are the foundation, then socks are the termites..er..skin..fabric that holds your toes together. If your socks get wet they become like chilled wet cement making you extremely miserable. Get socks that wick away water, keeping your feet dry. Better yet, get some socks that wick away insects, pet dander and social diseases. Socks come in all varieties, including peds, quarter, tube, and wind socks.

One argument to put to rest is what color your socks should be. I am told by someone who works at Nordstrom that the sock color needs to match the color of the trousers (and I assume here he means the outside color

Useless Knowledge: Imelda Marcos

Imelda Marcos was famous as the wife of Ferdinand Marcos, who became President of the Philippines back in 1966. Imelda is most renowned for her shoe collection, which was rumored to be as high as 3,000 pairs. She later claimed that she only had 1,650 pairs of shoes, which is much more acceptable. Imelda holds the Guinness Book of Records entry for the most pairs of shoes, but I know of several ladies who are making a run at that record. It won't stand long. The Philippines also holds the record for the World's largest golf event, which is an amateur tournament held in Baguio City every year. The event is a 72-hole tournament attended by over 1,000 golfers. If you took all the participants golf shoes and put them in a pile, it is still not as many shoes as Imelda owned. While most of the people who elected her lived in poverty, Imelda paid them back by spending lavishly on herself.

of the trousers), but I have also heard that sock color can be anything as long as they are not made of tin foil. Do what feels right to you. I can assure you that wearing tin foil socks does not keep your feet as fresh as something like Saran Wrap® does. Foil socks do make it easier for golfers with laser rangefinders to determine how far away you are.

Pants/Shorts

Please wear pants, especially the people who's belt is completely buried in a fold of skin created by a very large hanging belly. (Don't worry, the beer you consume has nothing to do with that condition, by the way) The name "pants" comes from the French word "pantaloons", which were ankle-length trousers worn in the 18th century.

Comfortable pants are key. There's nothing worse than taking a great back swing with a golf club or pitch fork and having your pants bind up and put pressure in sensitive areas. Well, there actually is something worse, and that is to walk backwards into a sharp barbecue fork left protruding from the shelf at the hardware store. It's that raw scream of pain that gets everyone's attention and makes the store dog bark. First aid kits are on aisle nine, but please no running in the store.

Any time I can, I like to wear dress slacks golfing. They look great, play well, and take attention off my swing. The PGA does not allow tour players to wear shorts and that might be a good thing. I am not sure I want to see some of those guys in shorts. Once you let them wear shorts, then next thing they'll be wearing flip-flops with spikes. We can't have that.

In the garden, if you are going to be doing lots of work on the ground, you might skip the cargo shorts and wear something long to protect your legs from the elements. I have found nickel, cadmium, and hydrogen in the yard and they are hell on your skin.

Belt

Steal my invention, please! I want to make a belt with a buckle that has one of those bubbles on it from a carpenter's level. The bubble would be placed on the face of the buckle vertically and would indicate when your belt buckle is not perfectly vertical. The purpose of this is to show that when the belt buckle is vertical, then you are probably in decent physical shape and looking smooth. Bravo, keep up the Pilates. If the bubble on the buckle shows it is leaning out away from your body, especially past fifteen degrees, you are overweight and need to slim down. If the buckle is past ninety degrees, then you have a weight problem need to lose some pounds, or up your life insurance, or both. We sell these belts on the web site for $350 each, made from the finest Corinthian faux leather hide material stuff. What a deal!

Shirts

Shirts, specifically collared shirts, are "de rigueur" for golfing just about anywhere. Many clubs and courses stick to an arcane rule about requiring a collared shirt. Why not require zippered pants? I am not sure what is more offensive, a person in a clean, uncollared tee shirt, or a person with a filthy wrinkled collared shirt that was bum rubbed by the owner's dog in the backseat of the car. A rule is a rule, I guess.

One thing that I have noticed about the shirts that tour players wear is that the shirts usually have a larger than normal logo on them so that the television camera picks it up. The best example is the polo shirt that Davis Love III wears - the Ralph Lauren Polo horse logo is so big on his shirts you can see the Polo horse's genitals. If those are the rider's genitals then that guy is not riding the horse properly. If horse racing does not pan out for the rider, he may have a career in those art films they make in Las Vegas.

Useless Knowledge: Pilates

Pilates is named after Joseph Pilates who started a studio back in the early nineteenth century to practice his central element of exercise - creating a fusion of mind and body. There are over 11 million people who practice Pilates and over 14,000 teachers. Many golf professionals take Pilates to build their core strength, and it does make a big difference in your health. I have been doing Pilates for over two years and it is great, although some of the exercises feel like they were designed at Abu Graib in Iraq. Put down your weights and take some Pilates classes, you will enjoy it.

One tip for the pros - if you are going to wear one of your sponsor's shirts that you just pulled out of a plastic bag, run some steam or an iron over it first. There is nothing more amateur than a shirt that still shows all the creases from packing.

Hat

If you stood on your head with a hat on, then your hat would effectively become your shoes, and we know already that shoes are required. That should end the debate about wearing hats.

Hats with built in beer bongs or those made from tin cans should be avoided on the golf course and in the garden. A hat's purpose is to protect one's noggin from the sun and keep the head warm in the winter. Phil Mickelson, who was known as the visor king on the PGA Tour, recently switched from his trademark visor to a regular cap hat. He claims that since his hair has thinned, he was getting a sunburned scalp all the time with the visor, so he switched to a covered lid so that he avoids a sunburn.

I am glad he made the switch because the visor has always been analogous to leather chaps for me - why not just wear a full pair of leather pants that cover everything if you are going ride a motorcycle or dance with other men to a disco beat? Same with the visor - it really shows a lack of commitment to headgear, and you never see anyone dancing with them on.

One of the modern trends today is for manufacturers to put their logos on just about every surface of a hat. There are logos that are seen on the edge of the brim of the hat, over the ears, on the back, and I am told some are going on top so the blimp picks them up. Maybe they should put the logos on the inside too?

If you are going to work in the garden, a hat is highly advised. If your neighbor Ferdinand (not Ferdinand Marcos, that dude is dead) is going to help, then maybe a helmet is required. Perhaps an explanation is in order.

One time I needed some help pulling out a stump left behind after a drunk driver crashed into the tree in our front yard. Uncle Mort was okay, but that was the last time he was invited over for New Years. He should have parked on the street anyway. I asked my neighbor, Ferdinand, to come help me remove the stump as I needed someone to do all the work. He agreed and pitched in to help but I was hoping he would take a more prominent role in the project, if you catch my drift.

At one point Ferdinand picked up one of those very heavy metal wrecking bars used to pry things from the ground and began tearing into the stump. As he was lifting and throwing the bar into the stump, he did not notice a hung-over Uncle Mort looking on and struck him in the cabasa with the other end of the wrecking bar. Thirty-two stitches later everything was fine, but a helmet would have protected Uncle Mort. In a odd twist of fate, Uncle Mort's scalp scar resembles the Nike Logo and I am envious.

Take a page out of Phil Mickelson's book and wear a protective hat when working in the garden or dancing with other men. Your scalp will appreciate it.

Gloves

As you may have noticed, most criminals wear gloves - at least that is what Hollywood portrays in the movies. Criminals know that there is nothing more comforting when stressed than a comfortable pair of gloves. I don't think it has anything to do with leaving fingerprints behind. One of the most famous glove/garden/golf stories is that of O.J. Simpson.

As you may recall, gloves were found near the scene of the crime and O.J. was asked to try them on in court to see if they fit his hands. In his best acting ever, he made it appear that the gloves did not fit. Johnny Cochran, the late defense lawyer, famously went on to say, "If the gloves don't fit, you must acquit". Truth be told by somebody, this was in fact an old saying that Harvey Penick, the great golf teacher used to say regarding

Useless Knowledge: Some Shakespeare

"Out, damned spot! out, I say!--One: two: why, then, 'tis time to do't.--Hell is murky!--Fie, my lord, fie! a soldier, and afeard? What need we fear who knows it, when none can call our power to account?--Yet who would have thought the old man to have had so much blood in him."

- Lady Macbeth

If you have to read some Shakespeare, read Macbeth, as it is one of his best pieces. Blood, murder, power, witches, but enough about the O.J. trial, In MacBeth, Lady Macbeth is distraught as she can't wash the blood off her hands after killing the King. Give it a read.

"I have never seen these hands before. Was that what I was supposed to say Johnny?"

golf gloves. Harvey meant that if your gloves did not fit, then you might as well quit. Johnny Cochran borrowed the line and this may have single-handedly (pardon the pun) won the case for Orenthal Julius Simpson.

Imagine, if instead, someone told O.J. the gloves were golf gloves, he would have pulled them on right away and asked where the first tee was. O.J. is an avid golfer and to this day continues the search for his ex-wife's killer on golf courses across the nation. Maybe when Scott Peterson gets out of prison they can go play Torrey Pines together and talk about how they loved their wives to pieces.

Besides serving as a pivotal turning point in a murder trial, gloves serve two purposes - to provide extra grip, and to protect the hands. Let's examine these in more detail.

The fundamental role of the hand is to grasp things, so anything that can be done to enhance that grip is welcome. When working in the yard one is frequently using tools that require a solid grip, and it is important to hold on. I once was swinging a landscaper's axe, and it flew from my hands and hit my wife's prized azalea. Luckily, she was out shopping so I was able to blame it on Ferdinand when she got home. Had I worn gloves, it would have been safer, and Ferdinand would still be allowed on our property.

Hand protection is of the utmost importance. Your hands are everything. The human race is defined by our hands and opposable thumbs. Manual labor refers to working with one's hands, so without hands we are merely intelligent weeds that are ambulatory.

You'll want gloves that are suited to the task at hand (again, my apologies). For digging and work with shovels, picks, etc., you'll need gloves that provide padding and some thickness to prevent blisters and injury. If you are just replacing some annual flowers, then some flimsy, cloth gloves are fine.

If you are trying to collect Panther Piss, then you'll want something that prevents bite injuries and can apply pressure to an open artery.

While gardening offers gloves of many shapes and sizes, we really only have one golf glove today, and we wear it on one hand. I am going to suggest to the golf industry that they market the following specialty golf gloves to increase revenue:

Other Hand Glove

This glove goes on the other hand as the name suggests. We typically wear a glove on the left hand (for right handed players) but nothing on the right hand, and this is a revenue opportunity for the glove manufacturers. All they need to do is come up with some reason why a right-hand glove is required and Boom! a whole new market opens. Everything is done in pairs and gloves should be no different. Maybe the other hand glove is required to prevent chafing when removing the left hand glove? It could prevent wood burns when placing the tee in the ground. Maybe the "other hand" glove adds thirty yards to your drives? Just get some pro to endorse it and everyone will be wearing them.

Sand Trap Glove

Wear this one when playing from the trap. It should be webbed between the fingers to more easily move sand from around your ball. The rules don't allow you to touch your ball in the trap, but I think it's okay with one of these gloves on. If your bunker shot comes out perfectly, you'll look like a bad-ass wearing the Sand Trap Glove, and if it doesn't, you can blame the poor shot on a worn out Sand Trap Glove.

Putting Glove

This glove includes some kind of slot that the putter grip goes into to provide perfect alignment and awesome feel. The glove might be festooned with some fancy looking graphics that give it an air of scientific legitimacy. This glove should be ultra thin and should enhance the pleasure of the stroke. It might be cool if it were ribbed as well. I think everyone would buy one, or at least keep one in the bag, just in case that special "who would have thought it could happen to me" opportunity comes up to use it.

Short Game Glove

This glove serves a unique purpose. When you are one hundred yards and in from the hole, use this glove to ensure a perfect shot with your sand wedge or lob wedge. This glove would be really thick so it feels like you are holding the business end of a baseball bat. The thicker grip would promote better control and would be just fine for choking that ground squirrel who has eaten a hole in your golf bag to get to your snickerdoodle cookies. Again, nice short game shots will be rewarded with praise like "great short game", and missed shots can be explained away due to using such a big thick glove.

Apres Golf Glove

This glove is pure style. You would put this on just after playing to allow your hands to relax and recuperate from a hard day on the course or in the garden. This glove would include features to massage the fingers and moisturize your damaged hands. It would have some small rubber grips to hold a cocktail or a beer in the bar. Not sure some of your homophobic friends would appreciate these, but be a rebel, and take care of your hands.

Confidence

Let's face it, sometimes confidence is all one has. Whether it's confidence that you'll stripe that three wood 260 yards over water to the center of the green, or confidence that you can outrun a family of raccoons after you take down their nest, you need the commitment of mind and body to succeed. It's all about confidence.

Candidly, I have never taken down a raccoon's nest, but I have one in the olive tree and the bandits are coming down at night and digging up my lawn looking for grubs and worms. This meal must be a delicacy for them, I suppose it is the equivalent of us humans going out for Sushi. In this case the meal is on me, or my lawn to be exact. Even though I have never taken out a raccoon's nest, I need complete commitment to the task or I am going to be eaten alive by some angry raccoons, and then suffer some of those painful rabies shots for weeks.

Speaking of bandits, it's interesting to note that there is a whole category of crimes called "Confidence Games" or cons, where people are tricked into doing things they would not normally do. So why can't some of the techniques of the con artists be used to improve our golf and our gardening? Well, for one thing, it is against the law, but only if money changes hands, so let's avoid that. Rather, let's adapt the con man's techniques to lawfully improve our golf and gardening.

Let's dissect what makes a good con, and then apply that understanding to improving our golf and gardening skills. Most good cons work by setting up a target or mark and having that person quickly build up confidence in the con man through some generous act. Examples include the con

Perhaps the greatest con movie of all time...

man loaning money to the target or performing some activity that would demonstrate the appearance of the con man's sincere and unwavering concern for the target's well being. You'll see this behavior sometimes from a neighbor who appears concerned that one of your trees is going fall over on your house, so he offers to have it trimmed at his expense. Later you find out he just wanted to hack it to the ground to improve his view of the beach. Good thing you are planting those fast growing Italian Cypress trees to block his view again.

Another example is when your trusted auto mechanic mentions that your car really needed a new fetzer valve, and he took the liberty of installing a new one for one thousand dollars. It's not so bad though as he performed the labor for free. What a deal! I trust that guy, but why are half his bottom teeth missing? If he is going to live a life of crime, then the least he could do is invest in a dental plan and get those choppers fixed.

These scenarios are in no way similar to the nice fellow I helped out from Nigeria who had several million dollars that he could not get out of the country due to some unfair banking regulation. He sent me an e-mail about it initially and we became great pen pals.

What a wonderful world we live in that a simple guy like me with very few shekels in the bank, can help a young Nigerian National get his millions out of his country. He offered to share some of his money with me for my kindness and assistance, but I insisted to help without asking for anything in return. *(Editors note - the Author provided his personal checking account info to help the Nigerian, and, in fact, all of the book sales revenue runs through the same account. It's odd that we have not made a dime off the book as of yet...)*

On a related note, April Fool's Day is a great time to try out some of these schemes with little fear of legal action. The trick for a good April Fool's Day gag is to misdirect the audience from the true ruse. For example, issue a press release which announces that Home Depot will no longer carry submarine parts or something like that. People will believe it and some will be outraged that Home Depot no longer carries the things they need.

Useless Knowledge: Nigerian Money Scam

The Nigerian Money Scam, and others just like it, start with a person receiving an email asking for help. The sender supposedly needs help in moving a large amount of money out of Nigeria, or some other country, in exchange for cash. These are all scams of course, and usually result in the unwary victim having their identity stolen at the least, and their cash stolen at the worst. The FBI advises you to contact them if you receive one of these letters. If you do have a large sum of money you need to move out of your country, contact one of these Nigerian Scammers, as they are obviously very effective at what they do.

The trick is to convince someone that you can be of help to them. Then turn the tables and ask for their help. This is when you take the money and scram. (we're not going to do that here.) Now that we are all skilled in the dark arts of the con man, let's finally apply these skills to golf and gardening.

So you are standing there in the middle of the fairway where you just crushed your drive. You are now looking into the mouth of the devil, and he has a 260 yard throat with a green at the end of it. It could just be a green olive he had for breakfast from this distance, but that's another story. How do you summon the strength, courage, and confidence, yes confidence (it's the name of the chapter after all) to reach down within yourself and hit the shot of your life?

If you have not figured it out by now, you simply trick yourself into believing you have hit the shot a thousand times already. Maybe you have hit that shot a thousand times; it doesn't matter whether you have done so in practice or in your head, you are ready. That's how Tiger hits them, how Jordan rained them, and why Steve Nash cut his hair. Steve's a good shot too, and I think his new haircut looks much better, by the way. You simply need to "con"vince yourself that you can do it because you have done it before. It may seem "con"trived, but it works.

In a recent tournament, Tiger hit his ball up on the roof of the clubhouse and he was prepared to go up there and hit the ball back down into play. He knew that he has hit a ball off every surface a thousand times and the roof would not be an issue. Tiger wasn't going to go up there, stand over the ball and then say to himself, "You can't do this.". No way, he was going to hit it flush.

Turns out he got a break and was given a free drop because something on the course was not marked properly. I was disappointed because I wanted to see a shot off the roof.

I wish on tour they would allow the "This doesn't count, but let me try it anyway" shot just for the viewers. After hitting his regulation shot, the player can indicate to his playing partner that he is going to hit this special shot. Give them each one shot per round. Then Tiger could go up on the roof and paste a ball down to the green. Wouldn't it be fabulous to see John Daly hit some shots that don't count? I can't imagine any more reckless abandon from him, but I am sure he would surprise us. This would make for some great television.

One time my neighbor Kirby hit a whiffle ball perched on his brother's head using a broomstick. Pure confidence! A grand full swing, and perfect execution. His brother needed four stitches to close up the wound, but you have to admire the courage and confidence of trying.

What about the phrase, "A leap of faith"? This is almost synonymous with confidence. Some shots in golf require a leap of faith to execute.

During a playoff with Tiger in China this year at the HSBC Open, Padraig Harrington hit a shot between the two trunks of a tree that was right in front of him. Harrington went on to win that tournament and later the British Open as well. (Actually, he picked Sergio Garcia's pocket on that win.) I am sure if he was asked about the tree in his shot line, Padraig would reply that he did not even see it, as he was so focused on the target. Anyone who lacked confidence would have not only seen the tree, but would have likely taken a ricochet into the potatoes for sure. Bad-ass shot by Padraig I say, and only made possible by confidence, with a little luck of the Irish thrown in as well.

After having watched some professional landscapers do some hardscaping (defined as something that appears hard so you need to pay lots of money for it) in my yard, I learned a few things.

Like Padraig Harrington, these landscapers cannot see trees. Seriously, they simply have confidence to do what they are being paid to do. I watched them build some forms for concrete and then mix and pour the gray batter like they were making breakfast cereal. It would have taken me a week just to plan it, and then I would be stressing about it the whole time. To them, second nature. Confidence!

Back to the raccoon family, I must admit that they are still living happily in their nest in the olive tree. I have not built up the confidence yet to get them down myself, although they had another feast on my lawn the other night with the full moon. I am building up the confidence to call a gardener, however, and let him get them down. He can take them to a nice raccoon farm in the country, where they'll live happily ever after. Actually, they'll probably just run from the nest, and move into my neighbor's yard.

Whether you are going after a cute family of raccoons who like worms, or you are going for that 260 yard approach for Eagle, be sure to have confidence in what you are doing. If you don't have confidence, you'll have rabies and a ball stuck in the devil's throat, and he doesn't like that.

Maybe you have never written a script for a PGA commercial before? Without confidence, you'll never try it. Take a look at my attempt at the end of this book. Maybe you have never worked as an agent for an aspiring author before and sold his book and commercial script for millions? All you need is confidence! Go out there and give it a try, nobody is stopping you but you. Start your career representing me, I dare you.

In a nod to Salvador Dali and his famous painting
"The Persistence of Memory" (1931) with the bent watches,
here are some warped golf clubs that Salvador might enjoy.
If this picture looks normal to you, give up drinking the yard chemicals
and come inside.

You can cut out this actual size horse shoe and hang it at your house for good luck.
If you do, you need to send me a check for fifty dollars, however.
Alright, go ahead and keep the it for free - See, it has brought you good luck already!

Luck

Regardless of any specific religion, I believe luck exists as a universal force that introduces random unpredictability to what otherwise might be a predictable outcome. What does that mean exactly?

Let me explain by example. You are playing exceptionally well and on track for a career round. You get to the eighteenth tee box and your insensitive playing partner reminds you that you are having a career round. This may be a passive aggressive move by him to sabotage your score, especially likely if there is any money on the line. Just as you start your back swing, a black crow comes down and takes a dump on your 460cc driver. It's too late and you skull your tee ball about forty yards, it hits a tree and comes flying back, luckily missing your beer to hit your loudmouth playing partner on the chin. Next time he'll shut the hell up and not remind you how lucky you are that you are shooting a career round! That's luck!

Another example of luck is when you are digging a trench in the yard to run some new sprinklers and you are swinging a pick with a full and mighty backswing. Just when you are almost done with the trench, the pick comes down and hits the gas line that was supposed to be buried twenty four inches deep. "What's that whooshing sound?" is quickly followed with, "GAS!", and then "call 911". The fireman always love to come out on a Saturday and help. The guy from the gas company loves it too. They always tell you how lucky you were that you were not smoking and then give you a bill for their time. There's luck again. Maybe I should contact my pen pal in Nigeria for help?

A great example of a climbing Bougainvillea plant, but also some fine construction work by Uncle Mort. If you look closely, that's a door in the middle of that wall. Mort took the children's phrase, "You make a better door than a window" to heart and put a door where a window should have been.

It seems like everyone refers to luck as either good or bad. You never hear anyone mention medium or neutral luck, because that might just describe what happens all the time. You might hear someone say, "He had really bad luck." or "She had phenomenal luck.", so there are varying degrees of good and bad luck. Let's talk about some as it relates to golf and the garden.

Your first thought might be, how does luck play a role in the garden? Most everyone understands luck on the golf course, but in the garden it seems like an odd concept. I, too, had a similar concern until it dawned on me that almost everything that occurs in nature, and in the garden certainly, has a high degree of luck associated with it.

Take for example the humble Bougainvillea plant that grows so heartily in Southern California. These plants offer spectacular, vivid color that make them look so wonderful (like the black and white photo to the left in no way demonstrates). Upon closer look you see that these plants have a nasty side to them. Their main branches are actually vines that have very sharp thorns, which by nature's design allow them to latch on to and climb things. These thorns also protect the plants from predators and golfers looking for balls, especially on the ninth hole at Glen Annie (www.glennanninegolf.com) here in Santa Barbara.

My observation of these plants is that they grow their vines several feet in the air and then they let the wind, gravity and other forces, most especially luck, determine where they come down. Once they come down, they begin growing and extending their vines until they are spread out like a giant spider's web. I believe the Bougainvillea is the garden world's equivalent of the sea's giant Octopus, with tentacles flying out everywhere. Equally as deadly too.

I pulled a vine down from a tree in the backyard that had climbed forty feet in the air. Talk about luck, after some very rigorous pulling, the vine came down and I sat to take a rest. In a great example of bad luck, I sat down on the vine and one of those sharp thorns found its way into a very sensitive place normally reserved for Doctor Messerlian's examinations. I let out a scream so loud that my wife calmly called the gas company guy back since she just figured I hit the gas pipe again. The Doctor said that a punctured colon is nothing to laugh about and that I was lucky I did not hit an artery. At least, if you hit an artery in that area, it's not likely you'll suffer brain damage, although my wife might argue differently. More good luck!

Another example in the garden of luck is how seeds move around and new plants grow. Some of you nature experts might say that the birds, the bees, and the wind move the seeds around, not luck. To some degree that's true, but let's focus in a little bit, maybe just on one bird, to see how luck plays a role.

Maybe the bird's daily routine is to get up around 6:00 am, sing a couple songs with his pals in the tree, take a bird bath, and then start his busy day of flying around collecting and eating seeds, some of which he drops, which hit the ground and begin germinating.

Maybe along the way he flies over the fourteenth fairway just when some fat guy pastes the drive of his life and the ball grazes the bird in flight. (By the way, that's the closest the guy will come to a birdie all year.) This throws the bird off course and he changes his route for the day. This leads to the bird picking up different seeds from different places, dropping some of the seeds in places that fate had otherwise planned, like right in the middle of my damn bougainvillea plant. The seeds fall through and a hearty Pitisporum plant starts growing underneath my Bougainvillea, and then with all the thorns on that plant, I can't get it out without further injury. So there's my misfortune of some bird having a bad day due to some fat guy on the tee. That is how luck works in the garden, at least my garden anyway.

What about luck on the golf course? Let's see, there I am swinging away and I paste my drive right down the center of the fourteenth fairway and this little swallow intercepts my ball flight and I graze the little fellow. (That was the closest I came to a birdie all year.) Luckily, my ball was slowed by the bird and it stopped before rolling into the barranca I never usually reach. I chili dipped my chip shot from there, but saved double bogey. It's always great when luck is on your side to save double bogey. How lucky is that? I could have had a triple bogey!

Most people who watch golf on TV can think of countless examples of luck playing a role in the game, so I'll skip those. What TV does not cover is all the luck that goes on behind the scenes. Take, for example, the camera man who is covering the fourteenth green at the Masters. Maybe the night before he got a little too aggressive with the chili fries at the local eatery, where it turns out the cook maybe was not aggressive enough with his hand washing. Next thing you know, the camera man has a stomach virus, and he has to call in sick. A backup camera man fills in and later gets struck in the head by a wayward approach shot from Davis Love III, wearing his giant Polo logo shirt with the horse genitals showing. Is this bad luck or just fate?

Regardless, the discussion so far had focused on the outcomes of incidents where some amount of luck is a key player. Is there any way the golfer or gardener can attempt to harness the power of luck? Some of us have already harnessed the power of bad luck, so maybe a revised question is how can we harness the power of good luck?

This pursuit has been going on for thousands of years, but there is hope. There are several good luck charms that you can employ to improve your game.

Rabbit's Foot

> The first is a rabbit's foot, which allows you to turn the rabbit's bad luck into your good fortune. Think about it, there are no references to rabbits in golf lore. So maybe the rabbit's foot is a great idea? Carry one with you and use it as a ball marker. I guarantee that your luck may not improve but the other players in your group will be so rattled that they'll miss their putts. You can also tee your ball from

a rabbit's foot standing on end. If a brush tee makes your ball go farther, imagine how much farther the soft fur of a rabbit's foot will help your ball fly! We're selling rabbit's feet on our web site for $395. You can buy unlucky rabbit's feet for $425. Give one of these to a friend, especially that cocky club champion who seems to have an unfair share of good luck.

If you find a rabbit's foot in your garden, it is either still attached to a live rabbit (lucky for him!) and he is hopping away from you or you have a dead animal on your hands. Do not attempt to remove the lucky feet from the dead rabbit in front of your children as they'll forever more consider you mean and evil. Do it later when everyone is asleep. By the way, rabbits like to eat roses (See the chapter on Rose Pruning) so they are not as cute as you think.

Horse Shoe

Another good luck charm is the horse shoe. Although not a great ball marker, the horse shoe can bring good luck onto the golf course. Carry a full set of four with you and feel free to break them out when waiting at the tee for that slow group in front of you to get off the fairway. Most tee boxes have a ball washer on a pole of some sort that makes an impromptu horse shoe pit. Try to ring the ball washer pole with the horse shoes. Have everyone join the fun, including the cart girl who likes to start her loud beverage cart just when you are about to hit your tee shot. I know a guy who had the horse shoes in his back pocket when an errant tee shot hit him square in the rear. The ball ricocheted off the metal horse shoe and hit his wife in the teeth. They had to stitch her jaw shut for a month. Now that's luck!

Horse shoes are good luck in the garden, for sure. If you find a horse shoe it is either attached to a live horse or you have a dead horse on your hands. It could also be that the horse was just lazy and they left their shoes lying about just like my kids do. It is tradition to hang a

Movie Review: The Cooler

This great movie came out in 2003 where the awesome William Macy plays Bernie Lootz, a person who's aura of bad luck effects everyone around him. He is hired by Alec Baldwin, who plays Shelly Kaplow, a casino manager. Shelly uses Bernie's aura to end the good luck of gamblers on a roll in his Las Vegas casino. (I hate it when they do that, I lost $2,000, in craps one time because they asked me if I wanted a drink and that broke my good luck mojo) The table turns when Bernie falls in love with Natalie, played by Maria Bello, and all his bad luck turns to good luck. Things get ugly, but end well, unlike in Alec Baldwin's private life with his estranged wife Kim Bassinger..

Useless Knowledge: Crickets

Crickets chirp at a constant rate depending on the species and ambient temperature. In fact there is a law called "Dolbear's Law" which provides the mathematical formula. According to Dolbear's law, it is possible to calculate the current temperature (in Fahrenheit) by adding 39 to the number of cricket chirps produced in fifteen seconds by the snowy tree cricket. They are now trying to teach crickets to chirp using the Celsius scale in the metric system but have so far been unsuccessful. Dolbear is lesser known for his law determining the day of the week by counting cat fights.

horse shoe (detached first from the horse) above a doorway at your house, but you can hang one in the garden too. They get rusty and take on a very weathered look. I like them because sometimes when you see a rabbit, you can grab the horse shoe and hurl it at the rabbit. Dead ringer!

There's some delicious irony there, catching a rabbit for his lucky feet by using the shoe of another animal. This reminds me of a local burglar who would break into cars by using a low-jack he had stolen from someone else's car. Classic!

Crickets

Turns out crickets are considered good luck charms in Asia and parts of Europe. We see crickets in the garden all the time and, of course, we hear them at night. Crickets make their sound by rubbing their wings together, much in the same way a large golfer makes that loud rubbing sound when his inner pant legs rub together. The cricket has two songs, a calling song and a courting song. Seems a shame that a critter gifted with a built-in musical instrument can only play two songs. I am not sure if a cricket would be considered a string, horn, or percussive instrument. I know when I step on them they make a cracking sound, which is definitely percussive.

Different cultures assign luck to crickets based on things like their color, where they chirp, and how they chirp. For example, in Barbados, a loud chirping cricket signals money coming in. If that were true, I would want as many crickets in my yard as possible. In fact, on our web site we're selling crickets from Barbados for $139 US each. We're not smuggling these into the country in our pants either, like the ill-fated monkey import scheme. These are legit with full papers. Believe me, the money will pour in when you set one of these on your stoop. Your neighbors will pay you to take the thing inside after just a few minutes. Buy a few and get me that much closer to affording my Cypress Point Club membership!

Many people have their very own good luck charms that don't fall into the traditional category. Uncle Mort plays the same lucky numbers each week in the California Lottery, but the numbers have not won him anything yet. I guess the numbers get luckier each week that he doesn't win using them.

People usually associate their good fortune with some inanimate object or "charm" that happens to be nearby at the time. For example, a guy bends over to pick up a matchbook and he finds a one hundred dollar bill. From that point forward he carries the matchbook with him because it brought him good luck. Maybe more good fortune comes his way. More money found, a new job, a lucky golf shot. Maybe later, much like the cricket, his legs rub together and the matches light in his pants. He then has to spend $375 in the ER to get burn salve rubbed on his loins. Was it good luck? Depends who is rubbing the salve, I guess. If it's Frank, the creepy night nurse, then it is bad luck for sure.

I have considered spinning out a separate chapter on Superstition because it plays such a large part of the modern consciousness. Maybe not so much in the garden, but certainly on the golf course.

Superstition differs from luck in the sense that with superstition you are usually trying to avoid an act in order to prevent a certain outcome, where with luck you are just hoping for good fortune. For example, the old child's superstition, "Step on a crack, break your momma's back" burdens the poor child to avoid cracks while walking, or his mother will end up in traction. If your Mom has a bad back to begin with, this is a horrible superstition. And we wonder why people end up in therapy.

There are so many common superstitions that sometimes seem so outlandish. For example, I read one on the web as follows, "Seeing a spider run down a web in the afternoon means you'll take a trip." Damn right it does, I am going to take a trip down to Home Depot and buy some spider spray.

When the summer comes here in Santa Barbara, we get these spiders that are as big as frogs. They like to put up these big webs to catch bugs and

Useless Knowledge: Elvis

Elvis Presley had an album titled "Good Luck Charm: Anything that's part of you" that came out in 1962. I am sure that Elvis felt some parts were luckier than others. If only he had owned a few of my lucky $139 crickets he might still be with us today...

Useless Knowledge: OCD

According to the National Institute of Mental Health (My alma mater), "Obsessive-Compulsive Disorder, OCD, is an anxiety disorder and is characterized by recurrent, unwanted thoughts (obsessions, golf) and/or repetitive behaviors (compulsions, golf). Repetitive behaviors such as hand washing, counting, checking, putting, chipping, driving, or cleaning are often performed with the hope of preventing obsessive thoughts or making them go away. Performing these so-called "rituals," however, provides only temporary relief, and not performing them markedly increases anxiety."

they scare the wits out of me. If I don't pay attention, it's easy to walk into one and then the giant spider is on my body somewhere. Where's that lucky matchbook when I need it?

I have heard countless stories of golfers with superstitions. Some are simple, like only using an English two pound coin for a ball marker to avoid bad putts. If this really worked, then wouldn't all the putts go in? I have a friend who believes that playing golf with his shoes untied will prevent a high score. This does not work, and worse, the untied shoes cause other unfamiliar golfers in our group to ask me if there is a charity they can donate to on his behalf. Tie the shoes and take a lesson, I'll pay for the first one. On the other hand, some superstitions are quite complex.

I knew one golfer who's superstition was that if he saw a lizard anywhere on the course, he had to catch it and eat the tail. He claims that if he did not do so, he and his family would go hungry. Wait, that wasn't a golfer, that was an Eagle. I have the Eagle confused with a golfer who thought lizard skin golf shoes were bad luck. I think he was right, at least for the lizard.

One excellent player I knew would only play golf on days with even numbers and he passed on the club championship because it fell on an odd day and he was superstitious about odd numbers. He always tried to birdie or bogey the par threes and par fives, and par or double bogey the par fours. This kept all his scores even numbers. This superstition went so far that he never wanted to win a tournament because he would be number one.

Turns out everything about his life revolved around even numbers and anything odd was to be avoided. He claimed that even the human body was evolved around pairs of key attributes. When I mentioned the brain and at least one other key part of the body that has an odd-numbered count, he mentioned that he had some surgery to eliminate some of the imbalances. That's taking it a bit too far, though, don't you think - skipping the club championship? To top it off, this guy's name was Steven. We called him "Even Steven"! I won't even tell you about "Odd Todd".

Useless Knowledge: Princess Grace

September 1982, Princess Grace of Monaco died of injuries sustained in a car crash near Monte Carlo. Here she is with Frank Sinatra right before she backs over the paparazzi photographer who took this shot.

Before becoming a princess, she was Grace Kelly, the American actress who starred in several Alfred Hitchcock movies.

It is rumored that her long scarf became entangled in the wheels of her car, causing the accident. Investigators later determined she was attacked by crazed seagulls, which caused the crash. I made that whole story up by the way, but it is no coincidence that Alfred Hitchcock is involved with both of these ladies.

There's a female golfer I know that insists on wearing a scarf while she golfs as she believes it protects here from flying animals that wish to attack her. (No need to worry about "Even-Steven" above attacking her I guess, now that he has had his surgery) Maybe she saw Alfred Hitchcock's famous movie "The Birds" and that started the superstition.
Well, her superstition may be spot-on because that stupid scarf has kept the birds, eagles, and albatrosses away from her golf scores, for sure. Every time she takes the club back, it always gets tangled up in her scarf and throws off her swing. She'll never score well with that scarf on. I have tried to gently point out that maybe the scarf is a bad idea, and she should switch to a nice bucket hat like Kirk Triplet wears. I also offered that, maybe, if she stopped wearing a worm costume when she played, the real birds would leave her alone.

As Stevie Wonder sang, "When you believe in things that you don't understand, Then you suffer, Superstition ain't the way". He could not be more right with that. The next time you play golf or garden with someone who is superstitious, consider yourself empowered to help rid them of their silly ways. Throw their lucky English two pound coin in the lake, record only odd numbers on their scorecard, tie those shoes, pull that scarf off that lady's head, and take those lucky matches out of your pants. But for God's sakes don't do any of these things unless there's a full moon.

Money

What good would a golf book, masquerading as a gardening book, be without a discussion of money? Money makes the world go around, it makes your garden look nice, and can help your game tremendously. The Beatles said, "Can't buy me love", but you can buy some golf lessons. Let's dig a little deeper.

You can't expect to improve your garden or improve your golf game without spending some money. Let's start with the garden and see where things add up. Before we get into the details, however, I want to point out that a major gardening project is in no way like a real estate transaction.

When you are involved in a real estate transaction, everyone who gets involved in the deal essentially walks up to you, reaches in your pocket, and takes some cash for some nebulous reason, and you are hamstrung to do anything about it. If you are lucky, they might say thank you. There's the title insurance people, the realtors, the home inspector, the termite inspector, and more recently, the Feng Shui Master. Everybody gets a cut, including the county assessor's office. What a racket! Fortunately, the situation is different for garden projects.

With a significant spend in the garden, you are in control, and you can even do some things yourself. Imagine in a real estate deal saying to the Title Officer, "You know what Tammy? We're simply going to skip the title insurance because I am going to do that myself." I just saved $2,500 and avoided the bogus fifty dollars for express delivery fees.

On your garden project, you can do almost anything yourself, armed with a little information and some confidence. If you are looking for "little information" this book definitely provides exactly that.

Before you start anything, whether its a garden project, a golf trip, or a real estate transaction, you need to create a budget. Many of you reading this may not have any idea what a budget is, so let me explain.

Some people will say that a budget is something like "money set aside for a project or expenditure". Others believe a budget is something only a business uses to keep track of their money. That dude on TV with the big teeth, Anthony Robbins, will probably tell you that your budget is unlimited, but I would suggest a more pragmatic approach.

Turn's out that "budget" is one of those 6-letter words, like "garden", that implies responsibility, patience, and discipline. With the concept of a budget understood, the next logical question is how do you put one together?

First, look hard at your own resources and figure out what you can afford to spend. Next, throw that number away, because you are going to go way over budget anyway. The true number you want is the number you'll get from your relatives, close friends, and neighbors, especially when you get halfway through the project and run out of money.

Be very careful when determining this amount, because there is nothing worse than having your landscape contractor knock at the door at 6:30 AM asking why your check bounced. He may have a special spot in mind on your anatomy to shove that small statue of Father Junipero Serra you just bought if you can't pay up.

Neighbors are a great source of funds for a project. If you tell them you'll take the car off the jack stands and put it back on the street if they could help pay for the new irrigation system, you would be surprised how quickly they'll cut you a check.

My neighbor gave me some cold cash to take down some trees that block their ocean view and I wonder if I should tell him that the trees are actually in the yard below me? I may send a letter to the guy who actually has the trees, demanding he take them down for free, since they are a nuisance. I don't think it wrong to apply the cash to my own project. It may take some time and some work, but you can raise significant cash in this manner.

If your neighborhood has a homeowner's association, then you can always look to them for cash. Put in a request for some money to beautify the neighborhood and then spend all the money in your own yard. You have to start somewhere. Those groups have no real legal teeth to sue you with anyway.

Back to the budget. You need to set one. No matter how big or small the project, you want to get the budget right so that you can have bragging rights. It is important that you go over budget so you can say you did, but you don't want to be too far off so that you look like a buffoon. Nobody is impressed by anyone finishing their project under budget. Here are some guidelines for setting the right budget:

Budget Guidelines:

1. What can you afford?

Take what you can afford and what you have raised from, oh, let's call it "fund-raising" from friends and family. This is your starting number. Take a moment to enjoy this number, as it will be the last time you'll be anywhere near it.

2. Develop a project plan.

This will cost roughly ten to 15 percent of the overall project. You can go without the plan, but you have no idea what you'll end up with. Imagine taking a trip on a plane that had no "flight plan" - who knows where you'd end up? Get a plan, you'll need it. This leaves eighty five percent of your starting number for the actual work.

3. European Influence

If you have anything Italian in your project, like sculptures, cypress, marble, or the Landscape Architect, multiply your starting number by one and a half. Worse, if the word "Tuscany" ever comes up, double your starting number immediately.

4. Permits

If your plan requires any kind of permit, then get rid of the plan and start over. Permits are expensive, take time, raise your property taxes, and come with all these pesky "code" requirements. So what if you have an electrical outlet under water in the pond? It kills the birds, and it will keep kids from sticking their hands in the fountain.

Getting a permit opens a can of worms with the neighbors, too. In most communities, filing for a permit sends them a notice and they have a right to get involved and offer their opinion. That's the <u>last thing</u> you want to do is give your neighbors the right to offer their opinion. You are going to get it anyway, but it is easier to ignore than when they offer it with the Sheriff standing behind them.

If they find out through the permit process that you are building and stocking a small lake for trout, they'll be all up in your grill. Avoid the nosey neighbors, unless they have contributed directly and like to fish for rainbow trout. On the flip side, if you get one of those notices from your neighbor announcing their plans to do something with a permit, consider it an invitation to visit them and ask them for something - cash, materials, golf balls, whatever. They'll appreciate your help in getting their permit approved expeditiously.

5 Hardscaping

Hardscaping is the work required to build garden structures like walls, paths, and large ham radio antennas. If your plan includes hardscaping, then you can apply one of these two budget factors: If your spouse will let you use old tires for a retaining wall, then cut your starting number in half, unless they must be Italian tires, like Pirelli's, in which case leave your number alone. If your spouse only wants the finest rocks imported from the Balkans, then file for divorce now and use your garden budget for your legal fees. If you can get by with concrete or some pressure treated lumber (which may shrink your gonads later, so wear gloves on both hands) then the hardscaping will represent about twenty five percent of your starting number.

6. Irrigation

Irrigation is an important factor. In this book, I have already advised that it is smart to tap into a neighbor's system where possible. It is better for the environment because you use less of your own water. Even still, you need to set aside some budget for irrigation work. This usually comes in around five percent of the overall budget, unless you design your garden like Uncle Mort.

Uncle Mort's idea of a great garden is one that is made up of two materials: Colored concrete and colored rocks, preferably all the same color - lava red. Mort's front yard is a driveway comprised of deep red concrete with the front yard area covered in those small red volcanic rocks. Uncle Mort's garden does not require any irrigation whatsoever since there is nothing to water. He did put in an extra hose bib on the front of the house that he uses sometimes to wash out the car when the dog gets sick inside. That only happens when they treat Spanky to a sandwich from Arby's on his birthday.

7. Plants and Shrubbery

Plants are expensive, but don't have to be. If you are like me and have shopped at the nursery, you already know how expensive some plant

Useless Knowledge: Caltrans

From their web site, "Caltrans manages more than 45,000 miles of California's highway and freeway lanes, provides inter-city rail services, permits more than 400 public-use airports and special-use hospital heliports, and works with local agencies. Caltrans carries out its mission of improving mobility across California with six primary programs: Aeronautics, Highway Transportation, Mass Transportation, Transportation Planning, Administration and the Equipment Service Center."

The people at Caltrans do a great job except when they close the one lane you need at rush hour, so they can erect a sound-wall, to keep people who live by the freeway from complaining that drivers honk their horns too much, during rush hour when Caltrans has a lane closure. It's like a flipping fractal...

species can be. Sometimes when you are out driving, you'll see some of these same expensive plants in people's yards, by the road, or just over the fence in that rich guy's yard. Sometimes there are more than enough of them, too many in fact, and it seems like it would be best for the plants to dig them up and take them home. There are two ways to do this:

1) In broad daylight, get yourself one of those Caltrans (See side note) vests, and a hard hat. Act with authority and remove the plant as if it is somehow adversely affecting traffic. Most people will leave you alone. Legal note - you can get arrested for impersonating a Police Officer but I am not aware of any law against impersonating a Caltrans employee. I am not a lawyer, however, so you are on your own.

2) If you want to do something good for nature anonymously, then you'll need to work in the cloak of darkness. Borrow your neighbor's truck and tell him it is for some charity work you are doing in the community to help youngsters get a better start. You don't need to explain that the youngsters are young plants and trees, he wouldn't understand. Park nearby your target and bring a shovel. If you are confronted by anyone, state sternly that you are working for CTU and that Jack Bauer needs the plant for an antidote he is making to save Audrey. Run on foot, leave the neighbor's truck; you can tell him it was stolen later. If you chose to buy all your plants instead then plan for spending 25% of your budget on them.

8. Furnishings

Outdoor furniture has become expensive and ridiculous. Look at any of the latest fancy catalogs from the companies that started out selling hardware and pottery, now they sell outdoor beds, rugs, and furniture - outdoor furniture that should be inside. There's a whole new category of furniture called "day beds" which are complete beds that are setup outside, with sheets, blankies, pillows, and everything. What happens when it rains? Who has the time to be sleeping outside in broad daylight in their day bed? When I was a kid the only reason the bed was outside was because it needed to dry out from somebody dreaming they were a noodle shooter. Don't get caught up in the appeal of fancy outdoor furniture, and don't buy those white plastic chairs either - those are strictly for people with RV's. If you are getting any furniture at all, add ten percent on to your starting number because the furniture is going to cost you. Damn outdoor pillows alone will kill you.

9. Electrical

Lights and electrical work are also key elements. Back in the day everything was "low-voltage lighting". Our voltage was always low because we never paid the power bill on time and Dad was convinced we were only getting ninety five volts instead of one hundred and ten. Today, low-voltage lighting is used to accent trees and plants and to keep people from tripping on the stairs made from old tires filled with cement. If you are going to use tires, be sure to put the white labels down, unless you want people to read "Firestone" on your steps. If your name is "Firestone" then maybe this isn't so bad. If you are thinking of cooking with the George Foreman grill directly on the patio, be sure to put in an outlet or two so you can cook those dogs up. Lights and electrical represent five percent of the total.

10. More Extras

Extra items like putting greens, horse shoe pits, trampolines, and so on can become major expenditures. You want to make sure you have enough space for these things and that safety is always a primary concern. Whenever safety is involved, so is more money. When we installed our trampoline it was going to cost another $180 for a safety net. My deductible on my health insurance is less than that, so I figured it is cheaper to simply fix a broken arm rather than prevent the injury in the first place. No matter how many surgeries or therapy sessions, the kids are going to remember that day on the trampoline when Uncle Mort jumped from the roof and sent all the kids flying. Priceless. By the way, not everyone was hurt and we saved money on the ambulance by having two people ride together. For any item that you add to the project like a trampoline, horse shoe pit, and so on, double the cost of the item and add it to your budget.

11. Facilities

Budget for extra costs, like portable bathrooms, and so on. There are always surprises when doing projects like these and when they happen, the best thing to do is to head for the portable bathroom. There's nothing that calms the nerves more than using the portable when your stomach is upset. You can always hose them out when things get ugly. The portable is great when you have workers at your house and you don't want them coming inside. Use it yourself - you don't have to take off your shoes when you go and the laborers will respect you for using the same facilities as them.

Extra facility expenses on projects are expected, so take your budget calculation so far and add fifteen percent.

12. Change Orders

In the spirit of Spinal Tap, this list goes one beyond eleven to twelve. Perhaps the most influential item in the budget is not one you typically call out, but we do so here - "Ch-Ch-Ch-Changes".

Changes have the greatest impact on the project budget. Your contractor has diligently worked up an exact price, you have agreed, and work has started. Just then, Joan Crawford busts in, like that horrifying scene in "Mommie Dearest" and insists that a window be installed, even though the location is in the middle of a bearing wall. Her poor husband, the CEO of Pepsi I believe, relents, and there goes his budget! The contractor loves it because now all bets are off. The CEO's fixed price project just went out the new window that Joan wants. The CEO of Pepsi soon dies and Joan takes over, but that's another story. See the movie, it absolutely ruined Faye Dunaway's career because everybody was scarred to death of her after that performance.

Sometimes it is hard to avoid making changes simply because nobody could foresee something before work started. Who knew that there was an ancient burial ground where the pool is supposed to go? It takes a special tractor to dig through these things and that costs money. Don't bother calling the local Anthropologist, by the way, he'll just want some cash to sift through the old bones, and will delay the project even further. Work quickly.

The best advice is to avoid changes at all costs. Even so, add thirty three percent on to your budget for changes.

So far this budget work up has been focused on things that add to the cost of the project. Aren't there things that can be done to lower the costs? In a nutshell, no, but here are some things you can try to do yourself that might help you break even:

1. Manual Labor

Manual Labor is one area where you might save some money. Be sure to know what your time is worth however. If a laborer is fifteen dollars per hour and you can make fifty dollars an hour selling Amway, then give up your Amway gig and do the labor. You'll just feel better about it, and your friends will start to call you again when the word gets out.

The problem with labor is that it is hard work, takes time, and is rarely fun. It is very hard to convince the kids that it is in their best interest to dig that one hundred foot long trench two feet deep, but it can be done. The nice thing about doing the labor yourself is that you get exercise, a sense of accomplishment, and some giant blisters you can show to people at work, who may offer to help when they see you're suffering. Decline their kindness and ask for cash instead.

2. Read Books

Read Uncle Mort's gardening design book. By using red concrete, some red volcanic rock, and some abalone shells, you can transform your yard into looking something like an underwater grotto in Bora Bora if you have your beer goggles on. His simple designs will save you lots of time and money.

3. *Punt*

Cancel the project. The best way to lower costs is to avoid them entirely. This may not go over big with everyone who has given you cash to start your project, but you can't always be popular. Keep the shades drawn and don't go outside unless you have to. Avoid everyone. If your spouse starts to give you pressure, tell her you'll start next week. This will buy you a few days. You can also pretend you need a permit and you are waiting on the building inspector to give you the green light. You can drag that ploy out for months, unless your wife is a building inspector.

4. *Use Cheaper Materials*

Remove any material from the project that can't be purchased at your local drugstore like Long's or Walgreens (My Mom got her medical degree there by the way). Some of the larger ones carry small plants and yard supplies., pots, fertilizer, etc. Don't go to Lowe's, Home Depot, Orchard Supply Hardware or any of the stores in that tier. They carry enough to get you in serious trouble and cost you cash. You may be able to get a lawn jockey at the drugstore, by the way.

5. *Exploit*

Use students, interns, and the like. Rather than use a fully licensed Landscape Architect, see if you can find someone starting out at a local school. Kids in junior high can draw some nice sketches, so see if you can get a class to do a project to draw out your new yard. You can save a fortune. Donate twenty five dollars to the school's glee club and you'll be a local hero.

6. Move

This sounds silly, but you can save a fortune by simply finding a home that already has the yard you want. Why spend $150,000 on a new yard when you can just upgrade to something else? Unfortunately, as I mentioned at the start of the chapter, real estate transactions mean people getting paid, so you'll probably end up paying six percent in commission, and other monies for moving expenses, termite inspections, home inspections, Cialis prescriptions, and so on. Your property tax may go up too, which is why you might need the Cialis. If these costs in aggregate are higher than your project cost, then stay put. If it is less, then move. If you have decided to move and you have already raised money from the neighbors for the current project, feel free to keep it, and consider it a going away present from them.

7. Scale back your plans

If your plan calls for a retaining wall that is four feet high and one hundred feet long, then consider building one with the first two feet made from concrete, and the top two feet made from hay bales. They are making houses out of hay bales now, and the only problem is keeping the farm animals from nibbling on them. Use this latest construction technique to lower your cost. Don't let anyone smoke near this wall. Save a fortune by building the entire wall with hay bales, but don't use it to hold back a hillside, nor put a fire pit nearby.

8. Get Creative

Consider using painted murals in front of your house. Put up some plywood and have natural scenes painted on them. Not those Greek nature scenes with nude people, but rather ones with trees, bushes, and animals. They do this kind of thing at retail locations all the time when they are remodeling the store. You are just going to make yours permanent, that's all.

Useless Knowledge: Hay Bale Construction

Straw hay bale construction uses baled straw from wheat, oats, barley, rye, rice and other material to construct walls that are then covered in stucco. These structures are inexpensive to build, and are easy to heat and cool due to their high insulation properties. It sounds like many of the raw materials are the same used to make beer, so worst case if your house falls down, you can simply turn it into beer and drink it. What a great use of natural resources!

9. Recycle materials from yourself and your neighbors

Remember the saying, "One man's junk is a another man's treasure". Most of the time one man's junk is another man's junk, but there are rare occasions when things work out. A friend of ours made two beautiful pilasters out of stacked five gallon buckets that graced the front entrance to their home. I would have taken the metal handles off, but they thought the handles added character. Use what you can and save!

10. Tint your windows

If you can't see the weed patch outside, you are less likely to want to go out there and spend money to fix it. Window tinting lowers your energy costs, keeps the house cooler, and makes it harder for people to see in when you are watching the NFL in your jock.

We have spent significant time discussing money and the garden. But what about golf? How can we budget and save money there? Let's see.

Just like with a garden project, you need to break things down for golf. Where are the major expenditures? Where can you scrimp? Where can you indulge yourself?

Let's answer that one right away - indulge yourself whenever you are a guest at someone's private club. Everything is on them, so have at it. There's nothing that shows more respect to your host then to pick up one of those expensive pullovers with the club logo on it. Wear it proudly. Food, drink, massages, golf balls, whatever, spend like there is no tomorrow, because you probably won't be invited back.

Insider's tip - get there early, long before your host and start spending. If your host had no idea you are going to be at the club a week early, charge everything to Mr. Underhill's tab, just like Fletch.

Golf Expenses

Golf expenses break down into these major categories:

- Equipment
- Green Fees
- Clothing
- Beverages
- Meals
- Club Membership
- Training Equipment
- More Equipment

Before we go through these one-by-one to get a sense of budget for golf, it is important to point out that golf is perceived as a game/sport that takes a great deal of money to get started. To this I say, hockey-sticks! You can start with a basic set of hockey sticks and use those for most golf shots and they are very cheap. You can also use them to prune trees as discussed in an earlier chapter. Seriously, golf does take a small investment to get started, but done wisely, you can get started cheaply. By far, the biggest investment you'll make in golf (and your garden) is TIME. Let's break the golf expenses down:

Equipment

Like any other activity, there are some basic things you need to get started. If you are a beginner, you can usually find someone who has some extra clubs and equipment laying around. Take them and use them and don't worry about the make, model, size, and so on as you'll rarely hit the ball anyway when starting out. If you are stupid rich, then go buy the very best, most expensive clubs; it's expected of you. Pick up a couple of our garden spreaders off the web site for $6,000 each while you are at it.

Useless Knowledge: San Quentin Prison

Besides being the venue for the live concert by Johnny Cash back in 1969, San Quentin has hosted other musical acts. In 2003, the band Metallica filmed a video for their song "St. Anger" there, and in 2006 the hip-hop group Flipsyde held a private performance for just the inmates. I am not sure who else they expected to turn up for that show actually. It's not well known outside the prison, but long time death row inmate rapper "Naughty Pine" performs shows inside, using spoons and a coffee can. Let's hope he gets a record deal in his next life.

No matter what your economic situation, you'll need a putter, some woods, some wedges, and a few of the higher numbered irons. If you are really new to the game, you may ask for a "hand wedge" at the local pro-shop, and they'll be happy to set you up with a pair. Don't buy the shoe wedges yet, those are for more advanced players.

To get started on the right foot, you'll also need a bag to carry your clubs. Like spare purses in any woman's closet, golfers always have an old bag laying around. I am not referring to one's spouse, I mean a golf bag. Pick one up and use that to get started.

A former co-worker, Josh Miller, used to tease me when I was starting out with golf, asking why I was using my wife's golf bag. That was because I had this hand-me-down red plaid bag that, in hindsight, was a little feminine. The red bag was also filled with some old Wilson Staff Blades that I had no business hitting, not because they were blades, but for another reason I would discover later.

One time at the range I was practicing with the almighty two-iron (before Tiger made these popular) and during a shot the club head broke off and went flying out into the range. I had the strangest feeling when this happened that my hands had just flown off, but was relieved to see that it was just my club head that was missing. With great embarrassment, I had to run out fifty yards onto the range to retrieve the decapitated club head. I took the club in for repair, where I was told by the club repair guy that I was swinging clubs with ladies shafts! Josh was right, I was playing with ladies clubs. I did two things right away.

First, I called my Dad to lambast him over the clubs that he gave me years ago. He interrupted my rant and asked me if I remembered the song "A Boy Named Sue" from Johnnie Cash. Of course I did, as Dad had a Johnnie Cash "Live from San Quentin" album that we used to listen to on a strange machine that spun black vinyl around and noise came out. In that famous song, Johnnie sang the tale of a man who's name was Sue, given to him by his dad who knew the boy would face a tough life without his dad around to protect him. Rather than give his son such a provocative name, the dad may have been a better father by helping to raise the boy and naming him 'Bob' or something more tame. Times were different then, and Johnny Cash had not married Reese Witherspoon yet.

Dad says he gave me the ladies clubs years ago to make me tougher in the spirit of the boy named Sue, so I guess I need to go find Josh Miller and explain everything. Maybe I'll just send him one of the crickets I sell on the web site for good luck.

The second thing I did was go buy some golf clubs for the first time in my life. I was almost forty years old and it seemed like a good time to make the step. I went to the local hot-spot in town for clubs, tried some out on the simulator, and then chose some sweet Ping I3's. The dude working there suggested ladies shafts, but I had none of it. Oversize grips, extended shaft, anything to make my clubs more macho. Instead of basic corded grips, I ordered bearded grips. Very macho indeed.

Once you have your clubs and bags, you need to get some golf balls. If you are new to the game, get the cheapest ones you can find, and try to label them with your home address, so people can mail them to you as you lose them, because you will. The best balls for beginners are used balls found on the course while looking for your lost balls. As long as you are in the deep ravine looking for your skulled tee shot, look around as there are bound to be countless other balls (and sometimes clubs) in there too.

You need shoes and a hat as discussed earlier, but these are not mandatory for the beginner. Shoes help you grip the ground better and keep you from falling off the planet when you take that giant back swing. A hat keeps your head from getting sunburned and can help those of you with abnormal skulls look like your head has a normal shape. Hats also hide your hairline. Ronny Howard looks almost normal with a hat, but when he removes it, his head looks like a pig's shoulder. Your hat needs to be a regular baseball cap style, bucket style, or something similar. Wizard hats, or anything that looks like the Pope would wear it, are currently not in vogue. The Pope is a five handicap I am told.

Movie Review: Night Shift:

One of Ron Howard's best movies of all time was the classic "Night Shift". This 1982 movie tells the tale of a milk-toast accountant, played by The Fonz, and a wild, hyper, over the top dude played by the yet unknown, Michael Keaton. This unlikely pair manage a group of ladies of the night. The movie is twenty five years old and looks it, but most of the humor is "genius". Shelly Long, more famous for her role later on the television show "Cheers", is also introduced in this great film. If you are at Blockbuster and they are out of the latest Bourne action flick, look for "Night Shift" in the comedy section.

Of course, you need tees, ball markers, shoe laces, and so on to get going, but you can beg, borrow, or steal these from just about anyone but the Pope. Does the Pope hit in the woods? Just ask the rabbit with the soiled fur who just met the bear on the log.

Green Fees

How much should you expect to spend on green fees? The simple answer is somewhere between zero and $500, using 2007 dollars as a basis. (If you are reading this in year 2500 AD, then golf probably costs a lot more and any jokes in this book about O.J. Simpson will mean nothing to you. There are people in the present day reading this book who find the jokes mean nothing to them as well.) Of course, free rounds are easy and have already been covered. The question may not be how much should one spend on green fees, but what should one expect for the money spent. Let me give you my take.

$0-$20

Expect lousy fairways, unhealthy looking staff, chipped paint, and junked carts. As long as the greens are okay, it may be worth the money. Don't be shy about cart stunts. You'll notice the surrounding real estate is zoned industrial.

$20-$50

Courses in this bracket should have the basic amenities and staff that are a little healthier looking. There may be good food available, a beverage cart, and some decent fairways and greens. You may be playing under an airport landing zone, however. Real Estate surrounding these courses is typically apartment buildings, light industrial, or possibly there is a sanitation treatment plant nearby.

$50-$80

These courses want to charge more but people just aren't willing to pay it, unless they are tourists. You may find a compressed air golf shoe blaster, and the cart guys may try to clean your clubs for a tip. Instead of cash, you might mention this book or the crickets as a nice tip. You might start to find better real estate around these courses, and it may be worth taking a look to see if there is a place your mother-in-law can purchase with rights to play the course.

$80-$140

These courses are going to be nice, but expect some attitude. They'll tell you when you are teeing off and they may mention some grade school geometry about a ninety degree rule or something for the carts. For this kind of jack there had better be free towels and water. They may have a nice locker room you can visit, equipped with some of that old blue barber shop comb cleaner liquid on the sink. That stuff tastes terrible by the way, but you may catch a buzz if you have no money left for beer after paying the green fees. These courses are surrounded by real estate you can live in, but the homes may be small and close together. Do not buy a house that is within range of a right-handed slicer off the tee.

$140-$250

Now we're getting serious. Anybody dropping this kind of glue for a round of golf is either on an expense account, or is not reading this book because they pay other people to read for them. Expect a free yardage book, a Starter who can speak English, and some very clean carts. The last round I played in this price bracket was $160, and the Starter decided to give us a course history before we could tee off. He went on to ask that we not hit Titanium woods from any of the wild grass areas as we might spark one of those famous California wildfires. Not likely, but Titanium woods can sometime cause a spark when they strike the ground or when you drag your opponent's driver behind your cart on the concrete cart path. Homes around these

Useless Knowledge: Titanium Driver Sparks

What on earth causes a Titanium driver to spark sometimes? According to the experts at Lawrence Livermore Laboratory, it has something to do with the rapid heat up and oxidation of the zirconium titanium glass in the driver. This happens during impact with the ground. What great news - tell your lady you are considering some zirconium for her. Go out and pickup that new 460cc Titanium driver, then put on a light show with it - you'll look like flipping Luke Skywalker. Swing fast and hard, just like on the course!

courses are very nice. Spread out, spacious, and expensive. Don't tease yourself by buying one of these homes unless you can afford the green fees, as you'll want to play all the time. If you insist on living there, find a rich neighbor who will treat you. If you can tie into his sprinkler system (covered elsewhere in this book) consider yourself way ahead.

$250-$400

These courses are most of the ones you see on TV, like TPC Sawgrass, for instance. If you want to save some money, just go toss some balls in the local pond at the park or local golf course. You're going to do the same thing on the seventeenth at Sawgrass anyway, so save yourself the money and embarrassment. Most of these courses are fantastic with excellent facilities and service. The courses themselves are top notch, which is why most amateurs shoot high scores. On a cost per shot basis, "going high" instead of "going low" may make more sense on these courses. It's a better bargain, you get more for your money. These courses are surrounded by "Estates", not homes, and you had better have some deep pockets. Just the utilities will eat up the common man's wages. Some of these people have so much money, they buy their gardeners memberships in the local country club. That's huge. Jango the day laborer has no shot at getting a membership from me anywhere.

$400 and up

Green fees in this stratosphere are reserved for the ultra wealthy who have their private jet parked nearby, or for those saps like me who are there for a "once in a lifetime round". Courses at this level include Pebble Beach in California, which is now up over $500 a round. My brother and I took my Dad there for his seventieth birthday a few years back and it cost a fortune with the green fees, caddies, food, lost balls, and the transmission in the Expedition I had to replace on the trip up there. Pebble Beach was fantastic, but they had just punched the greens so putts were falling even less than normal, if that is possible. Seems like they ought to offer a discount when the greens are punched but they don't. Maybe like next time I'll pay with my American Express card and dispute the charges if the greens have been punched.

I did manage to birdie the first hole, but that was the end of "going low" at Pebble. I guess I can say I was under par there, at least for a little while.

Expect every convenience at courses like this, including the best service, best conditions, and some fantastic golf holes that you will see during televised tournaments. Don't even ask about real estate around these courses as the properties cost more on average than what the Jerry Lewis Labor Telethon raised this year. If you buy one of these places, don't forget you have to furnish it. Don't think you are going to Ikea for the "Flingstrom" dining room table and matching "Dongfling" chairs. Nothing less than something from sixteenth century France will do. You're going to have fifteen gardeners and a staff of eight just to make your toast in the morning. If you are living in one of these houses, you have made it, and need to invite me over to play some golf with your gardener at his club. Maybe I'll bring Jango, the day laborer along.

Gambling

We've talked about Luck and Money, so the next logical topic is Gambling. Gambling is so prevalent in golf that it is actually mentioned in the rule book. In a nutshell, it's okay with the USGA to gamble as long as the wagers are informal and everyone consents to participate. Gambling in the garden is another story altogether, and we'll get to that.

One way to categorize golfers is by whether or not they like to wager when playing golf. I fall into the category of golfers who are so focused on the game of golf itself that I have no time for placing bets on my play. I feel like I take a gamble every time I go out to play on the course. Little do people within my shot range realize they are taking a gamble as well, when I tee it up. In fact, there are some courses in the Palm Springs area that have banned me from playing due to wayward tee shots. I have also been banned from any Sheraton property in Hawaii, but that is health related.

There are golfers who will bet on anything. I have seen people bet on what color the Gatorade is going to be when the cart girl pulls it out of the beverage cart. (It's usually orange, by the way.) I have also seen players tip the cart girl in the morning to make sure she pulls out an orange one at just the right time.

Others bet on the more mundane things like score, birdies, sandies, barkies, and so on, but these bets are boring and mundane. Let's consider some bets that you can use to add some excitement to your round:

Bet on who will be the first to mention a medical problem

The loser of this bet is the golfer who mentions some medical problem or malady that is preventing him or her from playing their best. "I would have nailed that five wood if it wasn't for that rash" or "I popped my wrist out arranging flowers, and now I can't putt straight". Listen closely, someone will always mention something health related, especially as you start playing with older golfers. Nobody ever mentions a physical condition in a positive light like, "Wow, I am crushing my drives because my peptic ulcer has tightened my core muscles.", You'll just never hear that.

Bet on who will wear the worst outfit

This may be easy depending on who you golf with. There are those players that dress impeccably on a regular basis, but sometimes have those bad days where colors clash and it looks like their dog dressed them. Other players dress like the homeless most of the time, but sometimes show up looking dapper like Bing Crosby, or the character Don Draper, on <u>Mad Men</u>, the hit AMC television series. This bet should be decided by the beverage cart girl. If she says "Orange", then she has screwed up the Gatorade bet, and needs a brain replacement, but we knew that anyway.

Bet on who's spouse will call first

This bet is easy if you know your playing partners well. Some spouses feel the need to check in every thirty minutes, while other spouses move out of the house and leave a restraining order behind. You'll know who to bet on; this one is easy. Don't bet on anyone who's spouse is playing in your group or deceased, you'll never win.

Bet on who will be the first to mention food

Again, fairly simple if you are playing with large people that are wearing ill-fitting hats. Around the sixth hole, these folks start salivating about the treats that await them at the turn. They'll start talking about all the shrimp they had the other night at the buffet, or

At the Pebble Beach Clam Bake in 1956, Bing Crosby, famous for singing "White Christmas", had a private moment behind a tree while curious people look on. What a performer. Mr. Crosby started the tournament way back in 1947, and the tradition has carried on since. His original tournament is now known as the AT&T National Pro-Am, played every February. His legacy is far more than his golf tournament, as he was directly responsible for the development of the post-war recording industry, and inspired other such greats as Frank Sinatra, Elvis Presley, Perry Como, and Dean Martin. Mr. Crosby is recognized as the most recorded human voice in history. I'll bet there are other sounds he recorded after a few hot toddies.

mention a new way to prepare meatloaf with melted cheese on top. Meanwhile, their game goes to hell and they lose all their focus. Three putts are common. This is a good time to wager more traditional bets with them, as you have the advantage. "Hey Louie, bet you ten dollars you can't hit that fairway". Strike while the iron is hot. If you have some food in your cart, show it prominently to improve your odds even more. Sometimes I bring some rolls from Cinnabon and heat them up with my laser range finder and the smell drives the heavies crazy. You can win big.

Bet on who will be the first to demonstrate anger

There's always that moment when everyone is having a great time golfing and someone hits a poor shot or has a bad break. At that point, the person does something obviously unnatural that demonstrates their anger or frustration. People will smash clubs into the ground, yell something profane, or perform some act of stupidity, that later they regret. I have seen Uncle Mort smash his four iron into a tee marker so hard that it exploded into pieces and he had to have shards removed from his lower extremities. Of course, he regretted that later. I have seen people break clubs, throw their balls, and kick things. How childish! If you are going to get mad, then break your playing partner's club, or throw their ball. It will scare the hell out of them and break any good mojo they have going, as well as set the tone for the rest of the round. If you really want to make an impression, lay on your back on the green and kick and wail like a two year old who is cranked out on powdered Enfamil. Get up laughing and everyone will think its a put-on.

Bet on who will be the first to blame a third party for a bad shot

"That flipping bird just hit my ball in flight and now I am in the barranca", or "I would have made my putt if those people behind us were not pushing us so much." "I wish I didn't eat those chili-fries at the turn, I can't relax when I swing hard." You'll recognize a phrase like this as soon as you hear it.

Bet on the first person to tell a joke, but it has to be very politically incorrect.

No clean "knock-knock" jokes here, it has to be something offensive. You'll know it when you hear it, because it usually starts with "Did you hear the one about the <insert racial, ethnic, religious, sexist, slur here> who..." blah blah blah. Sometimes, in spite of the political incorrectness, these jokes are quite funny, and we all need to be able to laugh at ourselves and blondes equally. You know who the normal suspects are in your group that like to tell jokes. If everyone betting picks the same person, then you can bet on what group he is going to offend, besides yourselves. If we ever play together, you can't bet on Uncle Mort. It's never a question with him as to whether or not he'll tell an off color joke, it's more a matter of how many he'll tell, and what group he'll pick on the most.

Bet on how far someone is going to slice their next shot.

This is a great mental game technique that from the moment you utter the bet, the player is already thinking they are going to slice it. If nothing else, it adds extra pressure to their shot. Never let the player hitting the ball bet on the worst slice, because odds are they can make that happen. These kind of bets won't make you popular, but sometimes you need an edge to win the match.

Not garden or golf related, but bet anyone you are with at the movies that there will be a helicopter appearing in one of the previews

Once you start looking for helicopters in movie previews, you'll be amazed by how many times it happens. There's always some action flick previewed, and when you have action, you have the whirly-birds. If there are no helicopters in the previews, then you might be at church.

What about bets in the garden? There are a ton of those. Let's take a look at some:

Bet your kids who can cut the lawn the fastest

They start this week and you do it next week. Of course, you can tell them next week that you lost their elapsed time, so they'll have to do it again. If your kids are smart like mine, they won't fall for this. In fact, my son keeps losing my elapsed time from last week, so I have to do it again and again.

Bet your neighbor that he can't prune your hedge in thirty minutes

Of course he can't, nobody can. But at least you'll get thirty minutes of work out of the guy.

Bet your neighbor you can dig up their pygmy palm and replant it in forty five minutes

Dig it up and bring it to your garden to plant. He'll think you are going to replant it at his house. Wrong! Go inside your house and close the curtains. Don't come back out for awhile. Let the dogs out in the yard to protect your new plant.

Bet your wife you can take a longer nap than her on the garden hammock

This is a great one if you are both tired; everybody wins.

Bet your friends they can't buy a copy of this book

This is a sure thing, just point them at our web site and make it sound impossible to get a copy. They'll take the challenge and maybe order two for good measure. These books are as rare as "Tickle Me Elmo's" after all.

The Masters

The Masters is without a doubt the greatest American golf tournament there is. Every spring we all look forward to seeing golf played by the world's best at that special course in Georgia, Augusta National. Everything about the place is phenomenal! The course is manicured to the finest detail, and the plant specimens are incredible. It is tough to decide what to focus on, the golf or the grounds.

Based on how immaculate Augusta National is, one has to wonder if membership requires personalities that are anal retentive? We already know you have to have money to join, but maybe every member has to sign an oath of Felix Unger-ism, the incessantly clean guy from <u>The Odd Couple</u>. (For those of you under thirty-five, see the sidebar on the next page for more information on <u>The Odd Couple</u>.)

It is rumored that Augusta National is only open for member golf play like three days a year, or something ridiculous like that. Every other moment is spent by the ground crew maintaining the gorgeous property. Gary Player recently stated that "If there is a golf course in Heaven, it is Augusta". If I get to heaven, I would like to have a course there that is open for more than a few days a year and I would like to finally see God hit a two iron.

Speaking of God and two irons, I am torn with a personal religious dilemma. One of the Ten Commandments states "Thou shalt not have other gods before me". I am known by friends and family for my worship of Tiger Woods. He may be godlike on the golf course, but I would not consider him a god in a spiritual sense. If there's something I need to

The Odd Couple

Felix Unger, played by Tony Randall, and Oscar Madison, played by Jack Klugman starred in the 1970's television adaptation of the hit Neil Simon Broadway play. Felix was the ultimate obsessive-compulsive anal-retentive while Oscar was the anti-Felix slob. Felix may have been Monk's father. The show was fantastic. By the way, Oscar was a sports writer who I am sure would have covered the Masters. Neil Simon's play is still running on Broadway.

pray about, it's not to Tiger Woods, so I think I am in keeping with the commandments, at least some of them. The important ones, anyway. For sure the first two...

I bet Tiger would give God a run for his money with a two iron in his hand on heaven's version of Augusta National. At the end of the day, I'll still pray to God for good shots from Tiger. I think that helps me keep it all straight.

Back to the Masters, a gardening golfer should watch the Masters tournament now with a different eye. Rather than just focus on the golf and the shot-making, pay attention to the exquisite grounds, trees, and flowers. You may have to wish that some of the players (lets pray not Tiger) hit some wayward tee balls into the forests and stands of trees and brush. It's then that you'll get a nice look at some of the species of plants and flowers. You may see Uncle Mort in there relieving himself because there are simply not enough rest rooms and his prostate is swollen.

Let me point out that the grounds keepers at Augusta National don't take kindly to some of the gardening techniques presented in this book. Just as you should show respect to others and only take their plants when they are on vacation, the same holds for Augusta National. If you are lucky enough to visit the grounds some day in person, don't touch anything. Come back at night when nobody is there if you wish to take some "samples" back to your own garden. How many people can say they have some dogwood specimens from Augusta in their backyard? Not this author actually, but not for lack of trying. During the hearing I told the Judge that I was taking the plants as part of the research for this book. While he still imposed the full fine for trespassing, he did offer to write a forward for the sequel to this book. Everyone's a comedian.

If Bobby Jones was the visionary behind Augusta National, Alistar MacKenzie was the scribe who captured Mr. Jones' vision and brought it to life. In Alistar's book, "The Spirit of St. Andrews", written in 1932, he mentions the thirteen principles of golf course design. (These are listed below without permission because I did not know how to get in touch with him.) I have added my own comments for each, trying to make these relevant for the gardening golfer.

1. **The course, where possible, should be arranged in two loops of nine holes.**

   When laying out your garden, divide it into halves. This makes it easier to always only be half done taking care of it.

2. **There should be a large proportion of good two-shot holes, and at least four one-shot holes.**

   This translates, of course, to lots of par fours and at least four par threes. Do the same in your garden - put in some plants that take a fair amount of maintenance, but also put in some easy plants too, like plastic plants or mature cactus.

3. **There should be little walking between the greens and tees, and the course should be arranged so that in the first instance there is always a slight walk forwards from the green to the next tee; then the holes are sufficiently elastic to be lengthened in the future, if necessary.**

   Alistar designed courses long before the easy-go golf cart. I suggest that had powered carts been available in his time, he would have added more areas for spins, donuts, and skidding stunts. His courses simply did not have space for these antics. As far as elasticity goes, plant a rubber plant or two, and you should be covered.

4. **The greens and fairways should be sufficiently undulating, but there should be no hill climbing.**

   Again, there were no powered carts then. Had there been carts, Alistar would have added hill climbing as an activity. Nothing better than a good hill climbing competition with a golf cart. Take your clubs off the cart first, in case you roll over backwards. Leave your playing partner's clubs onboard, however, as you'll need the weight in the back.

> "Most golfers have an entirely erroneous view in regard to the real object of hazards. The majority of them simply look upon hazards as a means of punishing a bad shot, when their real object is to make the game interesting."
> Alistar MacKenzie

This is the new electric car that was purchased by the Augusta National Golf Club in Augusta, Georgia, for Bobby Jones to use to get about the course, March 19, 1953. This shot was taken right before Xzibit and the dudes on "Pimp My Ride" got a hold of it. Now it has some deuce-deuces and a 42" plasma with a kicking bass.

5. Every hole should be different in character.

I have played many rounds and seen some people's character change dramatically from hole to hole. Sometimes, all it takes is one bad shot and your kind playing partner turns into what can only politely be described as that part of the anatomy directly under a horse's tail. Seems just about every course designer shared the different character principle, because I have seen this happen to people no matter what course I have played.

6. There should be a minimum of blindness for the approach shots.

Even then, Alistar was politically correct, thinking of the blind golfers to make the courses he designed work for them. Bravo!

7. The course should have beautiful surroundings, and all the artificial features should have so natural an appearance that a stranger is unable to distinguish them from nature itself.

This description is fitting for most cosmetic surgery as well. On the golf course, it's hard to disguise the fourteen CBS broadcast tractor trailers as pine trees, but Alistar thinks you should try. In your home garden, follow this principle. If you have an ugly utility pole in your garden, either cut it down, or hide it by painting it the color of the sky.

8. **There should be a sufficient number of heroic carries from the tee, but the course should be arranged so that the weaker player with the loss of a stroke, or portion of a stroke, shall always have an alternate route open to him.**

I like the idea of heroic carries, where a pasted drive off the tee can find the green. With my game, I always take the alternate route, which usually means playing up a parallel fairway. In the garden, heroic carries usually happen when I try to carry all my tools, lawn mower, and garbage can at the same time. This usually leads to a hernia, so take the alternate route and only carry what you can in the yard at one time, unless you like Frank, the Creepy Night Nurse giving you an examination in the ER.

9. **There should be infinite variety in the strokes required to play the various holes-that is, interesting brassie shots, iron shots, pitch and run up shots.**

I have seen many players whose strokes appeared to be infinite, one bad one after another. This usually led to the change of character that Alistar mentioned earlier.

10. **There should be a complete absence of the annoyance and irritation caused by the necessity of searching for lost balls.**

This may be one that Alistar never really achieved in his course design. In spite of his best efforts, people still get irritated and annoyed when having to search for their ball that missed the fairway. So make the fairways super-wide. In fact, just blend them all together where fairways run parallel to each other. That should provide a complete absence of annoyance.

11. *The course should be so interesting that even the scratch man is constantly stimulated to improve his game in attempting shots he has hitherto been unable to play.*

    I am not a lawyer, but when someone uses the word "hitherto" I get nervous. Translated to garden design, be sure your garden is interesting no matter how often someone visits. I like to hide a beehive or small rodent to make things exciting for visitors.

12. *The course should be so arranged that the long handicap player or even the absolute beginner should be able to enjoy his round in spite of the fact that he is piling up a big score. In other words the beginner should not be continually harassed by losing strokes from playing out of sand bunkers. The layout should be so arranged that he loses strokes because he is making wide detours to avoid hazards.*

    Wow! The player should enjoy the round even though they are piling up a big score? "Enjoy" and "big score" are two phrases that never go together, unless you are enjoying your opponent piling up a big score. Not sure how this applies to gardens, just don't leave things in piles, unless it is a compost pile.

13. *The course should be equally good during winter and summer, the texture of the greens and fairways should be perfect and the approaches should have the same consistency as the greens.*

    Exactly. Same holds for the garden. Everything should be perfect no matter what the time of year. Different parts of the country have local techniques to guarantee this. I have been to some areas where this is achieved by filling the entire yard with concrete, which stays perfect year round. Other locations fill the yard with alternating areas of white and red volcanic rock, although that does require some occasional weeding.

Inspired by Alistar, here are thirteen of my own design principles and course ideas: Keep in mind I have never designed a course, so I am only qualified to offer these simple suggestions:

1. Have plenty of rest rooms.

Take the expected average age of the golfer and divide that number by 10. Use 18 holes as the numerator and the number calculated above as the denominator. This is how many holes there should be between rest rooms. For example, if the average age is going to be sixty, divide that by ten to make six, and divide that into eighteen. The answer is that you need one rest room every three holes. If you serve breakfast burritos, put an extra rest room between holes three and four and have plenty of towels on hand regardless of the age of your golfers. If you know some of your golfers are using Avodart or some other drug to reduce prostate size, you may get by with fewer rest rooms. It's not an exact science really, but be sure to take local conditions into account.

2. Allow golf carts in the parking lot or onto public streets.

There's nothing better than pulling up to your car to load your bag straight in. Even better, is to take your cart for a spin on the local thoroughfare. You'll be the hero at the drive through Starbucks if you come by in a golf cart. Patrons will applaud you. Recently, Bill Murray made some friends in Sweden by driving a golf cart on public streets. He may have been drunk, however. Too drunk to drive a car he claims.

3. Get rid of the ninety degree cart path rule.

I can argue that no matter where I am on the course, I am ninety degrees to a cart path somewhere. It's a mathematical law I believe

Useless Knowledge: Dogs and Calculus

As long as we're discussing fancy ninety degree mathematics, it is worth mentioning a great story about a dog using calculus to his benefit. Timothy J. Pennings, a Mathematician in Michigan, studied his dog's behavior when retrieving a stick thrown into the water. The dog always chose the most optimal route to fetch the stick, considering distance and speed. Mr. Pennings confirmed this by performing calculus computations for the optimal route, and compared these with actions of the dog. Canines can't actually do calculus because they can't hold a pencil, or operate a scientific calculator, but they do have some innate sense to do things in the most efficient way. Next time you do some calculus, keep your dog nearby, they may be able to help.

that no matter where you are, there is something around the corner at a ninety degree angle. I am more in favor of a rule I'll call the "fifty percent" rule that says you'll attempt to stay on the cart path fifty percent of the time. People understand percents better than degrees, and fifty percent is easy. How many things do you see on sale for ninety degrees off? None, but people understand percents better because they deal with them everyday. Just to clarify, my fifty percent rule does not mean that you drive with two wheels on the path and two wheels off.

4. *No waiting for the green to clear on short par fours.*

Play always slows when some clown thinks he can hit his new driver onto the green 325 yards out, and everyone has to wait for the green to clear so he can try. Most of the time they never make it. Allowing these "long shots" will speed up the group on the green anyway, because they don't want to get hit. Besides, there's so many doctors on the course that if someone gets hit, they'll be taken care of right away.

5. *Implement the "Gimme Ring".*

The Gimme ring is a two foot diameter circle painted around the hole. If your ball is touching or inside the ring, you add one to your score and consider the shot holed. This speeds up play considerably. No humor here, they should just do it. Purists be damned, there's nothing pure about a dude who just finished covering his entire yard with red concrete, coming out to the course and insisting that he sink every putt to complete his round of 131.

6. *Always have a stunt hole.*

Alistar mentioned heroic shots and this principle takes that to an extreme. Just like the windmill on the eighteenth hole in mini-golf, you need a hole people will talk about. Whether it's a tee box two hundred feet above the green, or a fairway ten feet wide, make things interesting. Throw in a par 7 hole and eliminate a par three. Think of all the maintenance you save. In Idaho they have greens only

Not a proud moment for George C. Scott at Cypress Point Golf Course. Everybody gets gas, but showing off is something the real General Patton would have never done, especially with ladies around. Had there been more rest rooms on the course, this may not have happened.

accessible by a small boat. How about a tree in the middle of the green? Riviera in Los Angeles, home of the Nissan Open, has a sand trap in the middle of the seventh green. Why not a tree on one of your greens? Do something crazy, the Tour pros love that kind of thing.

7. Add a food court and shopping.

Just like they built the Disney World monorail through the hotel in Orlando, Florida, run some of your holes through shopping and food areas. You can mingle with the patrons, see the kids, and enjoy a quick Panda Express plate between holes. Factor this into your rest room calculation, however. If there is Indian food available, double your rest room calculation for all holes after the food court.

8. Move the course closer to low flying aircraft.

For some reason, just about every golf course is in the flight path of an airport somewhere. If you are going to endure the noise from these flying machines, you ought to at least have to deal with the wake of the planes too. Position your course so that most of the holes are right at the end of the runways, so that when planes come over they are no higher than fifty feet or so. The air coming off these jets is impossible to predict. Local rules may allow you to replay a shot that hits or enters the aircraft.

9. Get great staff.

This may be more a staffing issue than a course design principle, but don't hire anyone who looks like they suck on lemons for fun. Courses should be staffed with happy, cheery, people who inspire you to play better and enjoy yourself. Moreover, if they have a relationship with the local authorities that is even better. Taking the golf cart on the freeway seemed fun, but nobody expected to get pulled over. Staff can help get you out of those kind of binds.

10. *Always have the range close to the first tee.*

In fact, I would suggest the first fairway and range be combined so once you hit a good one, you can just say, "I'll play that one" and go hit your second shot. People can wait as you play through and it works out well for everyone. Courses without a range are the best candidates to implement this upgrade. The old excuse that there is not enough land doesn't cut it, especially if you take my advice and combine the first fairway with the range.

11. *Course layouts should change daily.*

There's nothing more exciting than taking the course layout and changing it entirely every day. Yesterday's par three is now a par five, and the green for hole number two today was yesterday's eighteenth. Golfers will be confused at first, but they'll appreciate the variety. Score won't mean anything anymore because nobody will be able to figure par. People always play better when they are not keeping score.

12. *Allow two groups to play the same hole at the same time.*

The FAA allows parallel runways at airports, so why not parallel tee boxes? Just like with the FAA, only in the fog or severe wind should a parallel tee box be closed. This will speed up play dramatically. The course design needs to support this style of play, but I think it will work well.

14. *Get rid of hole number 13.*

Some buildings don't have a floor number thirteen due to people's superstitions (covered in the "luck" chapter earlier). Hole thirteen is usually where I make the assessment as to whether I want to knuckle down and finish well, or take the cart and look for a hill to climb. If my score is already near the ambient temperature, then it is time for cart stunts. Getting rid of hole thirteen means I need to make the assessment at hole twelve, which leaves me more remaining holes to get my act together or more time for cart stunts. If it were up to "Even-Steven" introduced already, there would be no odd numbered holes and you could play thirty six holes every time you played.

Etiquette

Eddie Cut - Who the heck is that? When I was a kid and I heard Dad talk about "Eddie Cut" I thought it was a reference to Uncle Eddie's gas-passing or an injury of some sort. I would learn painfully, later, what it meant to golfing and gardening.

Without looking it up anywhere, the word "Etiquette" to me invokes the notion of following simple norms and behaviors that usually bestow kindness or respect on someone else. (Uncle Eddie's wind is at the opposite end of any scale that includes etiquette.)

How is it used or applied? Here's an example. On the golf course, when someone is getting ready to pull out their wallet and buy you a drink from the cart girl, it is proper etiquette to accept their kindness and get some of those expensive cashews, too. It's rude to do otherwise. If you don't spend a lot of their money they'll be offended because you might think they are cheap.

When a fat guy gets ready to hit his tee ball, it is proper etiquette to laugh or snicker when he takes his waggle. This is a queue to him that he needs to lose some weight. I can't think of a kinder act. When a player drains a giant putt, it is proper etiquette to grab his ball from the hole and throw it in the nearest water hazard and yell, "Would have been great if you did not cheat". Wait for a second to check his reaction, he may confess, he may not. If not, then say, "just kidding" and offer to buy him a new ball. If he confesses, ask for at least fifty dollars to keep quiet. These are the social norms people expect to happen on the golf course. Local customs may vary, of course, depending on where you live.

You probably have not spent much time thinking about it, but etiquette is useful in the garden too. When you have hired someone to rip out your ivy, it is polite to offer them camomile lotion at the end of the day, right before you mention that it was poison oak they were working with. That is just plain polite and kind. Don't shake hands or accept any hugs from these people, as you may get exposed to poison oak yourself.

Don't confuse etiquette with manners. There are some subtle distinctions worth noting. Etiquette is a french word, based on the word "quette", which is also in the word "bri-quette", which is, of course, used as the fuel for barbecuing. Manners are the first thing to be dropped at any family barbecues that I have been to, and I am not aware of any French food that is prepared on the barbecue.

You'll never hear an old woman say, "Mind your etiquette", nor hear a Frenchman say "Rue d'la chat qui peche", which loosely translates to "why doesn't your cat have manners? He keeps licking the salt off my ankle" (very loosely, I might add)

Etiquette and manners are really about respect. By behaving according to expected social norms, one demonstrates respect for themselves and those around them. Undoubtedly, you have heard the phrase "He was dissin' me", slang for "He was disrespecting me". Nobody wants to be disrespected, which is why Rory Sabatini likes to speed up slow players. It's about respect.

Many of the youngsters coming of age have sadly been brought up without any real exposure to proper etiquette. Let me give some examples of recent and flagrant violations of proper etiquette both on and off the course by these future leaders:

Young men showing bare mid rifts when golfing

It's fine for women with "darling figures", as Mom would say, to wear just about anything they like, but men should not wear anything that shows bare skin below the arms. It's not dignified. Some of the up and coming younger players like Camillo Villegas and others like to show their pilates six-packs when playing. Tuck in those shirts, start acting like men, and drain some putts. Imagine what Fuzzy Zoeller must be thinking when he sees these guys.

Hats worn sideways, backwards, or just improperly

Wearing a hat in any other manner than it was intended is simply an act of disrespect. Imagine, for a moment, Abraham Lincoln wearing his stovepipe hat cocked to the side. How silly would he look in photos? He would look like flipping Willy Wonka, played by Gene Wilder, in the original <u>Willy Wonka and the Chocolate Factory</u> movie. Maybe if Mr. Lincoln had worn his stovepipe hat cocked sideways to the theatre, Mr. Booth would have either missed, or been so disrespected that he would have left in disgust? We'll never know for sure, but hats should be worn properly or not at all.

I do wonder if stovepipe hats will make a comeback? Imagine all that space for the golf equipment manufacturers to put their logos and images on. In fact, they could cover the hats in LCD material and have them display constantly changing images and video. (If anyone is doing a "prior art" patent search for such a hat, let this paragraph serve as proof that the idea was mine first.)

Letting a group play through

This is the norm in Europe where smaller groups play through larger groups on the course. They call a twosome a "two-ball" in Europe and they call a one-ball "Uno", "Lefty", or "Mr. Right" just about everywhere. Any time you have less balls playing up on more balls, the more balls need to let the less balls pass. Unfortunately, this courtesy is rarely honored, and golfers, especially the Brits, get angry. No

Famous People: Abraham Lincoln and Jim Furyk

I couldn't help but notice the striking similarity between Abraham Lincoln and PGA Pro Jim Furyk when researching this book. They both have the same nose it appears. I hoped to show a photo of each below to demonstrate this, but I could only afford one licensed picture. Instead of Jim Furyk, I have included a picture of some toothless guy, so you'll just have to use your imagination.

matter how many balls you have, always let faster moving groups play through. It's polite, shows proper etiquette, and shows you have balls. If Tommy John shows up, let this "three-ball" play through, even if he is by himself.

Cell Phones on the Golf Course

Back in the day the golf course was a place where people went to escape phones, process servers, the law in general, and pesky bill collectors. Things have not changed much since then, but now phones have found their way onto the course in numbers. There's nothing more annoying than someone missing their putt because a cell phone went off, and then claiming that because the phone was mine that they should get a take over. If you allow this rule exception, it is not called a "Mulligan", but a "Cell-Again", meaning you get to hit it again because a cell phone went off. "Rubbish", I say. Keep cell phones off the course and save your calls for later. One kind thing to do is to offer to hold everyone's phones until after the round. When play gets slow, sneak away and use them to dial those 976 numbers you heard about in the barber shop. When the guys get their bills a few weeks later, they won't remember a thing.

Stepping on someone's putt line

Many youngsters are simply not aware of this important protocol. Since they usually weigh so little when young, it is normally not an issue, but when "Little Johnny" explodes into "Big John" in his teens, the footprints on the green can be menacing. There are two actions required here. First, Big John needs to drink water instead of soda pop, and he needs to learn where to walk on the green.

One trick my Dad used to teach me not to walk on other people's putt line, was to ask me to freeze when I was standing on his line. He would grab his seven iron and hit a low punch shot off the green right at me. I learned real quick how to navigate the green properly and Dad honed his seven iron punch from a tight lie. The greens keepers disliked Dad for this teaching, but he insisted it was for the good of the game.

The next step beyond etiquette would be couth, defined as "showing or having good manners or sophistication; smooth." This is taking etiquette to the next level by introducing sophistication. Since this book is hardly sophisticated, we'll save couth for the next book.

Turns out the software I am using to write this book (Wordstar 2 on an IBM PC Junior, if you must know) is flagging the word "couth" as being unrecognized. Clearly, the publisher of the software has no couth whatsoever. No wonder they are no longer in business.

Useless Knowledge: IBM PCjr

This "breakthrough" computer was shipped in 1984. The $1,200 version had 128K of RAM, and a 360K 5.25 inch floppy disk. This machine had joystick ports, fancy graphics, and a powerful speaker. To put things in perspective, your cell phone probably has one thousand times the capability of the "Peanut", as it was called back then. The first Apple Macintosh shipped in January of 1984, after an unforgettable commercial which aired during Superbowl XVIII. Microsoft won't admit it publicly, but the XBOX 360 design is really based on the feature set of the original IBM PC Jr.

Charity

Giving back, that is what it is all about. Most sports, especially golf, are deeply involved with charities. I can't think of a nobler act than to help a charity spend their money. It takes a lot of hard work and many hours of thankless effort, but in the end, the payoff is sweet - nothing better than a trip to France paid for by the United Way or the Red Cross. This is all tax free, of course!

It has always been interesting to me how most tournaments that benefit a charity are really simply a trade - the charity provides some golf and tee prizes, and participants, usually corporate sponsors like title companies (who just fleeced me), will pay a higher green fee in exchange for a tax deduction. If we can drag along some visitors from the Japan office, all the better. So if the green fee is two hundred dollars, and the charity nets forty dollars per player, why not just give the charity one hundred dollars directly and cut out the golf? Because you jack-ass, it's really about the golf.

Don't get me wrong. I think the contribution to charity is fantastic and there's no way I would stand in the way of that. In fact, the only standing I would be doing is in line to sign up for any charity event where golf is involved, and someone else is sponsoring me.

I will say that most amateur charity events are scramble format, where the foursome uses the best shot all the way into the hole. Most of these tournaments are won with scores around fifteen under or so. There is some great strategy you can employ to either win the tournament, or have a great time, or both.

The first thing to do is to take an honest assessment of the players on your team. Check out the other players apparel, equipment, and shoes, especially the shoes. If their shoes are brand new, then they probably play little golf, and think that a scramble format has something to do with breakfast. If their shoes need polish and are worn on the toe tops, then you have a superb golfer on your hands. Good golfers wear out their shoe tops because they finish their swing properly , with their weight on the front foot and the rear foot on the toe.

You'll be able to tell right away who the real golfers are from the corporate hacks who might get a ball in the air if they are lucky. I am not trying to be a golf snob, but you have to determine your teams strengths and weaknesses. If it looks like winning the tournament outright is going to be five times harder than "shooting the moon" in the card game "Hearts", then the next best thing you can do is to distract the other teams.

First, have your best player hit a safe shot, and then have the others play with reckless abandon, more so than usual. Don't be afraid to hit wild tee shots into other nearby fairways, or use a four iron when a lob wedge will do. This rattles the players on the other teams. While I would never advocate damaging a course in any way, it might be fun (especially if you are the first group) to bring along some landscaper's paint and paint new hazard boundaries on the course for those playing behind you. Make that water hazard extend half-way out onto the fairway, right where the slicers always hit it. This works best if you are the first group out. Everyone may laugh about it later, if you choose to tell them or get caught.

No matter what the tournament outcome, the end result is fabulous. Golfer's were able to do what they love to do and some money was raised for charity. How perfect is that?

What about charity in the garden? Letting the ground squirrel live another day, rather than bashing his head in with a low iron does not count as charity. By the way, never give a ground squirrel a break, nor give a cab driver a break; neither one will ever return the favor.

Most charity work related to gardens revolves around volunteer work - you know helping the local church fix the rose garden or helping the grade school garden project plant some of those special "weeds" that Neil Young likes. Another example is when you get to clean up the highway as part of your community service work, related to your conviction of growing the wrong plants in the grade school garden. At least, they did not find the monkeys in your pants!

Helping with gardening in the community can be very rewarding. Sometimes I would go out at night and contribute by removing pesky stone statues, trees, and shrubs from properties where these things simply were not needed or appreciated. It warms the heart, really, to bring home a rare garden statue and put in my yard where it will be cherished forever, or at least until some other guy sets his sights on it.

One charity I am big supporter of is F.L.F.B., (See our web site for Tee shirts!) which stands for "Free Lobsters From Boiling". This group buys live lobsters from restaurants, runs them outside before they are cooked, and then frees them out in the mountains and fields, allowing them to enjoy nature as it was meant to be. We could return them to the ocean, but they'll just get caught again, so the high-chaparal is a much safer choice. Their chances for survival are not as good as in the ocean, but the odds are much better than being tossed in a boiling pot of water. Besides, after thousands of years they'll adapt and evolve, and hopefully grow wings or paws.

I am sure that if you asked lobsters if they would rather boil in a pot of water or go hiking on dry land, they would chose hiking. (Lobsters may be hard to communicate with. I am not sure if they bark, growl, or make any sounds at all.) Give to your local charity, and next time, pass on the lobster.

Just so this book has some appeal in Europe, we added this photo.
The sign says, "Do not play behind this line".
In spite of this player's ignorance of the rules, he is putting with a left hand low grip, nice!
Note the well manicured plants and the challenging course layout.

Rules

A game without rules is a meeting, a ruler without rules is called a stick. No book on golf is complete without some discussion of rules. No discussion of gardening, without saying the word "hoe", and giggling would be complete either. Surprisingly, there are rules to follow in the garden and, of course, there are rules to follow on the golf course. Let's talk about golf rules first.

If you have not already purchased a USGA Rules Book, you should do so right away. (We sell a version with some of the key pages cut out for $12 on our web site) There is so much to learn about how to properly play the game and ensure that at least, when you break a rule, you do so knowingly. In my mind, it's not about breaking the rules, it's about avoiding them entirely.

It's one thing to play a non-comforming ball that goes 400 yards intentionally, it's quite another to have some "rules-nut" tell you that you cannot ground your club in his trousers, at least not while he is wearing them. I only attempted to ground my club in his trousers (from the backside) after he accused me of using a non-comforming ball, which I was. It wasn't about the rule; I just did not like his tone of voice, that's all, which is more about etiquette in the end.

Anyway, the rules of golf are quite amazing. While there are some very arcane and bizarre rules, most of them all make total sense and really are not that hard to follow. When you consider all the potential things that can happen on a golf course, the USGA and their brethren at the Royal and Ancient (R&A) have done a tremendous job to cover just about any rules scenario you could imagine. There's only thirty three rules to follow. Get a Rules book, crack it open, and learn something about the game.

I had a situation come up where I learned how to properly apply the rules. I was playing in my local club's annual championship on the par five tenth hole when my cart mate determined that he and another player in our group had played each other's ball on their second shot from the fairway. Since neither was playing so well, they both agreed to just hole out with the other player's ball. They asked the rest of us if that was okay. We sheepishly agreed, thinking the decision was immaterial because everyone was playing so poorly. Big mistake!

No sooner had we finished that hole than my cart-mate catches fire with his clubs. He proceeds to roll six birdies on the back nine and is later crowned the winner of our flight.

His win was bittersweet, as he left the awards ceremony right away knowing that his win was hollow. He was also parked in a red zone, but it's just as well he left. Somebody was going to mention the rules infraction if he hung around. "Take the money and run", I say.

After, I explained to my golf coach and good friend Doug Crane, PGA Professional, what happened. He gave me some great advice that I would like to pass on - whenever a situation arises where there is any rules question about what to do, simply say, "I wonder what the rule book says about that" and then get the rule book out. Don't say, "I think you are breaking the rules" or "Cheater-Cheater, Pumpkin-eater" and then get into an argument.

Had we handled the situation properly, my cart-mate might still have won, but he could hold his head high knowing that he followed the rules. He later asked if I had slashed his car tires, but I would never do that. "Let's see what the California Penal Code says about tire slashing"...

As most of you already know, there are plenty of rules in golf that cover just about anything, but there is one in particular that is quite noteworthy - Rule 1-3 - Agreement to Waive Rules. Here is the rule verbatim,

> "Players must not agree to exclude the operation of any Rule or to waive any penalty incurred."

This rule speaks to exactly what happened to me in the story above, but it is so much more than that, because I'll argue that rules are waived all the time.

Most golf is played with friends out to have a good time. So your friend shanks a ball into a hazard and you tell him to simply hit another one. By the rule, you both should be disqualified (DQ'd) for this. Some pros call getting disqualified a "Dairy Queen". Wow, sounds harsh but the rules are the rules. Of course, you are probably not in a tournament situation, but if you are going to agree to waive rules, then why not allow the shoe and hand wedges to be used at any time? It's a slippery slope when you start breaking the rules. Unfortunately, I am struggling to twist this discussion into something humorous, although I have struggled for the entire book to do so, you might be thinking. So let's change direction slightly.

There are a few changes to the rules of golf that I think should be considered for the next rule book. Here they are:

1. Rule 4-4 Maximum of Fourteen clubs

If the golf industry wants to sell more clubs they need to allow more than fourteen in the bag. Imagine having a 7.25 Iron, and 7.50 Iron, and a 7.75 Iron. Let's face it, I can't hit the regular seven iron straight so the extra clubs are not going to make any difference. Most amateurs are the same way. Let people have fifty clubs if they want; it won't matter and the equipment makers will be happy.

If you want to limit the number of clubs, I suggest a more equitable approach where different clubs have different point values and you can't go over a certain number. For example, a driver might be one hundred points while a wedge is only twenty points. Add them all up and stay under 1,400 or something if you like the number fourteen

There's way more than 14 clubs in that bag, as it should be using the Blair Club Scale. The craps stick is a great to use when your putt has gone long and you need to pull it back into the hole. Come on Yo Eleven!

so much. I will say that a Ball Retriever should count as a club, at least four hundred points on what I'll now refer to as the "Blair Club Scale". My reasoning is that a club should be defined as anything you would swing to defend yourself against an attacking bird or fowl.

A ball retriever fits this definition, but so does an umbrella. I have never seen anyone hit a golf ball with an umbrella, but I did see an old guy battle off an attacking black bird with a Titleist umbrella. The bird won and the old guy needed to be put down, and I always wonder if he is in heaven right now wondering if he should have used his ball retriever instead.

2. Rule 6-4 Caddie.

The rule says that you can only have one caddie, but I think more should be allowed, like an entourage rather. Imagine what some of the celebrity Pro-Ams would be like if Snoop Dawg could bring along his possie. The more the merrier, I say. I think play would speed up too if people were allowed to dance.

3. All Rules Regarding "Relief"

I think that anytime you need to relieve yourself, you ought to. It's just not worth risking the inflamed prostate. I can't tell you how many times I have ruined a round because "relief" was not allowed. There's pressure, and then there's bladder pressure, which is far worse. "You can't swing freely when your feeling pee-ly" as Grandpa used to say.

Ok, so maybe we're not talking rules here but perhaps course etiquette covered elsewhere in this book, but there are some hard and fast rules about relieving oneself on the course. Let's consider a few...

- If anyone can see you, don't go, unless it is an emergency.
- Never urinate in long trousers unless you unzip them first.
- Never urinate on anything that is on higher ground than you are.
- If you have to do anything other than urinate, leave the course as

Useless Knowledge: Rule of Thumb Phrase Origin

Some believe the origin of the phrase "Rule of Thumb" comes from an English law that allowed a man to beat his wife with a stick as long as it was no thicker than his thumb. I am not sure if other parts of the anatomy were considered as the gauge before the law was passed, but maybe the thumb was the thickest body part they could find in England at that time. Remember, this was long before Tom Jones came on the scene. Turns out there is no serious evidence that this was ever a law in England, and the more common understanding is that the phrase comes from the practice of using one's thumb to measure, estimate, or align things. Catch your lady giving Tom Jones the "thumbs up" in Las Vegas, and maybe you should get out the broomstick. They may not mind in England.

there is nothing dignified about a golfer creating a divot in their pants. However, if you have an emergency like Larry up at San Geronimo in Northern California, grab as many towels as you can and head for a deep bunker. Use the rake when you are done - not a rule, but common courtesy. Kick your shoes when your come out too.

- No waggling. Some men, particularly when they have a great round going, may celebrate with a little by waggling while taking relief. I have seen people fooling around, swaying, and shifting and it always ends in trouble. One time a player in our foursome at Pelican Hill in Newport decided to relieve himself near a cliff and he started waggling. Turns out the dirt gave way and he tumbled down a steep ravine, ironically right into an area where golfers frequently relieved themselves. That dude was unhurt, but pissed.

If you really want to have some fun with the rules, you can leave the rules alone, but change the definitions that proceed them.

For example, the USGA has a definition for a "Lateral Water hazard ", which includes note #1 that says, "Stakes or lines used to define a lateral water hazard must be red." Well, there you go - what if the stakes are a sun-faded pink color? No more hazard as far as a strict interpretation of the rules go. Ground your club, take practice swings, play with abandon, you are not in a hazard!

There's also the definition for "Abnormal Ground Condition", which you can redefine for just about any situation. Say your ball lands in a tree and there is no way to climb the tree, well, that sounds abnormal to me. Who has trees you can't climb? Drop another ball with no penalty!

What about rules in the garden? We have all heard our Dad yell, "Don't run with the sharp hedge clippers!" or "Don't touch dead birds!" or "Don't self-emoliate yourself near the hay-bale retaining wall!" but are these really rules for the garden?

Remember a rule is a principle or regulation governing conduct, so we need to understand proper conduct in a garden setting. But here's the deal. Unlike the golf course where there is expected "conduct", there's no such requirement in your own garden. Do what you like, when you like. Plant whatever you fancy as long as it brings you joy and makes you happy. But don't self-emoliate yourself next to the hay-bale wall, Dad would be angry.

Statistics say that when you prune a tree with a bag of golf clubs, a hockey stick, a whistle, and Pabst Blue Ribbon Beer, injury will result 98% of the time. However, if you climb a tree with just the beer, injury will still result 98% of the time. By those statistics, it is safe to prune a tree with your golf clubs. Just leave the beer on the ground.

Statistics

Lies, damn lies, and statistics. There is no greater game for statistics than golf. Think about all the "stats" we have to consider - fairways hit, greens in regulation, putts per green in regulation, Tiger's winnings, driving distance, and the count of tiny carrots consumed at the player buffet. That's not true, nobody counts those carrots except Hazel, the observant waitress at East Lake in Atlanta. One time she saw Lumpy take one too many and she added some eye drops to his iced tea. Soon after he had what can only described as an urgent deuce on the par three second hole. He definitely flushed it.

The PGA Tour has a whole section of their web site dedicated to statistics. Statistics are defined as "the science that deals with the collection, classification, analysis, and interpretation of numerical facts or data, and that, by use of mathematical theories of probability, imposes order and regularity on aggregates of more or less disparate elements." That's all good and well, but let's get right down to it. Modern television sports broadcasting uses statistics more than just about anybody except the folks in Vegas. In fact, three out of four commentators use statistics at least once per minute of air time. What a stat!

Everybody understands statistics like, "Tiger is eight and zero when leading a major after the first two minutes", and these are acceptable to most of us. Where things get dodgy is when a stat is presented that ties together seemingly unrelated facts. For example, "Jim Furyk hits all greens in regulation when he plays with Gold Bond medicated cream applied", or "Ernie Els wins all his Ryder Cup matches when his caddie hasn't brushed his teeth.". These are tough to swallow, and we sometimes

Green in Regulation Defined

A green in regulation (GIR) is when you are able to get the ball on the green and still have two putts left to make par. So if you are playing a par five, you need to be on the green in three strokes to record a green in regulation. GIR's are a leading indicator of who is going to win a tournament. If you are the worst putter in a scramble foursome with Stevie Wonder, Ray Charles, and Helen Keller, then GIR's are not going to help you that much. You always need to get the ball in the hole in two putts or less. Try to get as many GIR's as you can, but more importantly focus on getting the ball in the hole.

feel like the commentators are stretching to say something, or anything. The statistics give them something to say when there is nothing to say. How about some stats on how often the commentators are wrong about something?

Having said all of that, there are some very cool statistics, and some that are quite enlightening. One of the most amazing, in my opinion, is the Scoring Average that the PGA Tour publishes. At the time of this writing, or perhaps at any time, Tiger leads with an average of 68.04, with Ernie Els a full shot behind with a 69.08. In years past, the gap between Tiger and #2 was sometimes just one tenth of a stroke! I am not sure how they are keeping score, but how do you win by one tenth of a stroke? These guys are good, and even though Tiger wins many tournaments, the margin between the top players is slight.

I keep statistics for all my rounds using software called Intelligolf (www.intelligolf.com). The product is very powerful and it can chart all the key stats one needs to improve his or her game. I have learned that if I can hit more than fifty percent of greens in regulation, I can shoot in the seventies. If you really want to crunch numbers, putts per greens in regulation is another telling stat. From careful analysis, I have also learned that if my Dad has blueberry pancakes before a round, ninety five percent of the time he will need an Alka-Seltzer by the turn. "Plop-Plop, Fizz, Fizz, oh what a relief it is."

Statistics in the garden? Here is an interesting statistic related to the garden. A new market research study by the National Gardening Association (www.gardenresearch.com), Residential Lawn and Landscape Services and the Value of Landscaping, found that homeowners spent a record $44.7 billion to hire professional lawn and landscape services in 2006. Wow, that is serious business!

Recent statistics indicate that approximately thirty billion dollars a year is spent on golf, including equipment and green fees. If you were to take a ratio of money spent on landscape services as compared to money spent on golf, right now that ratio looks like 1.48, meaning that for every dollar spent on golf, $1.48 is spent on landscaping services. Armed with that statistic, I want to change the title of this book to "Golfing for Gardeners" as clearly there is more money to be made from landscapers, then from golfers. (It's really not about the money for me, however, it's about the cash.)

Imagine all the money to be made selling grips, gloves, shoes, and swing trainers to the guy out there digging up your sprinkler system! As soon as Nike comes out with a line of athletic landscaping clothes, they'll make it big. Get Michael Jordan and Tiger (and me) to pose mowing a lawn or pruning and Nike will own that market. I dig it.

On Statistics..

"Say you were standing with one foot in the oven and one foot in an ice bucket. According to the percentage people, you should be perfectly comfortable."
~Bobby Bragan, 1963

In Summary

I hope that you have found something of interest here that you can apply in the garden, on the golf course, or purchase on our web site.

Some say that in life, "It's what you leave behind that is important", and I think I have spent too much time on that topic for this book. Maybe the next book will be better? "But how could it not be better?" you might be thinking. No matter, this book will serve as part of my legacy, along with the Superfund Cleanup site I managed for awhile.

No matter what your passion, the garden, the game of golf, mink undergarments, or all three, never waiver from your love for these things, and continue to try to be the very best at them. You may not be the best in the world, but you'll be far better off than the person who did not even try. Hopefully, you are glad I tried to write this book.

If you see a lonely lobster wandering in the high chaparral, give him a little water, and move him to the shade. Do the same for me, if we ever cross paths in the future. I hope we do sometime soon.

BONUS MATERIAL NOT FOUND ON THE DVD

We don't have a DVD,
but if we did, this material
would not be on it

August 25, 2007

Peter Blair
Reference Golf
1039 Via Los Padres
Santa Barbara, CA 93111

Mr. Blair:

I am sorry to inform you but your patent application for the following invention has been denied:

MEASURING THE QUALITY OF THE SHANKED SHOT - APPLYING IMPACT TAPE TO GOLF CLUB HOSEL

We realize that you see value in being able to best judge where on the hosel exactly your shanked shot made contact, but there is prior art that indicates your idea is not unique.

Impact tape for the golf club face has been around since 1923 (USPTO #276-678) and your patent simply allows the same tape to be applied to the hosel. Not only is your idea infringing on someone else's patent, we and the other golfers here in the office wonder why in the name of God do you need to measure impact on the hosel in the first place? Shouldn't you just go take a lesson? Please don't appeal our decision, it's final, and your idea is laughable.

Best Regards,

Frank Dogsanis
US Patents Office
Washington, DC.
(USGA 4.2 index BTW)

Reader Survey Card

We really appreciate your feedback to make our books better in the future. Please fill this out honestly and completely, and then hold onto it in case we need it later.

What did you like about the book?

What was the best part, besides getting to the end?

Were the golfing/gardening tips helpful?

Should the Author write another book?

Would you recommend the book to others?

What did you not like about the book?

What was the worst part of the book?

Were you offended more than eight times?

Where do you keep the most valuable thing in your house and when do you usually go out?

Script for TV Commercial

What follows is a script written for the PGA to use for one of their self-promoting commercials. It is hoped that with the success of this book that the author will be allowed to direct this fine quality vignette. Enjoy the show!

PGA Logo used without any permission whatsoever.
Our hope is that someone contacts us from the PGA to complain, and we can then use the opportunity to pitch the commercial. Right now they won't return our phone calls.

COMMERCIAL SCRIPT FOR PROFESSIONAL GOLFERS ASSOCIATION OF AMERICA

Pitch: This commercial brings the audience into what appears to be a thief's final instructions to his team before a big heist. It appears that the target is an armored car carrying a large cash payload, but, in fact, it turns out to be a range tractor loaded with golf balls. The robbers are really just trying to get some range balls for free. This commercial has the feeling of a big crime going down.

OPENING SCENE	Scene opens with two men and a woman in a SUV going over the final steps before the "big heist". The men are "special forces" looking, the woman very pretty.
Leader:	I have been working for months on this heist and today's the day when the big payload is on board the hardened steel vehicle. The job must go down flawlessly or this will be our last hit. Does everyone know their part?
All	Yes (in unison with a touch of humorous boredom, as if they have practiced this for weeks).
Leader	Do we have the iron?
All	(Unison) Yes
Leader	Synchronize Watches!
All	Done!
Leader	Put on your gloves and let's go…(All put on golf apparel, hats, gloves, shoes, and so on. These should be black in color in keeping with the perceived spirit of the task at hand)

NEXT SHOT	The SUV pulls up to a gorgeous club house and parks right at the driving range.
Leader	We're within range. Target identified
ACTION	The pretty woman gets out and approaches an oncoming range tractor coming up to unload, and it's bursting with range balls. The tractor stops (some balls spill) and she talks with the driver (who is Carl Spackler-esque, Napoleon Dynamite like, or a college punk kid) As this discussion starts, robber golfers emerge from SUV in the background with clubs (the iron) and bags and sneak around behind the golf tractor. They begin to unload range ball buckets and run them over to a vacant tee box at end of the range. This is done with some military precision. This is the big heist going down. While this is happening.....
Pretty Lady	Do you give golf lessons here?
Driver:	(Confused) Er, eh, No, Yes. What do you need to learn?
Lady	(Seductively) I have trouble with my stroke. I can't seem to find the length I am used to.
Driver	(gulps...)

ACTION	As she states this, she is keeping one eye on the theft of the range balls. The driver is clueless as the lady mesmerizes him. Once the balls have all been stolen to the range, the robbers smile and start hitting balls. The lady abruptly ends the conversation, smiles towards the range tractor driver, and walks away towards the others. Just then, many of the other golfers reveal themselves to be FBI on a stakeout (no guns shown). Walkie-Talkies and wrist communicators are used to announce the big heist has gone down. Robber golfers take off onto the range itself but slip on range balls on the ground and get hit with flying balls. FBI pursues. Nice chance for some good slip and fall stunts, maybe in slow motion..
NEXT SHOT	The bruised robber golfers are handcuffed and led to a FBI van. The Leader is overheard talking to the other robber golfer
Leader	Do you think they get the golf channel in prison?
	In the background, the word "Fore" is yelled by someone... Final action is single range ball striking the van near leader and rolling along the ground in front of him.
Golfer #1	Back to the range a beginner says to another, "Why did you yell "Eight"?
Golfer #2	The reply, "because I thought I was going to hit two people and eight was easier to yell than fore twice"
FADE OUT	Fade out to "Golfers will do anything to play more golf. PGA Golf"

Here's the author and his son Anthony starting work on the next book, "School Projects for Golfers".

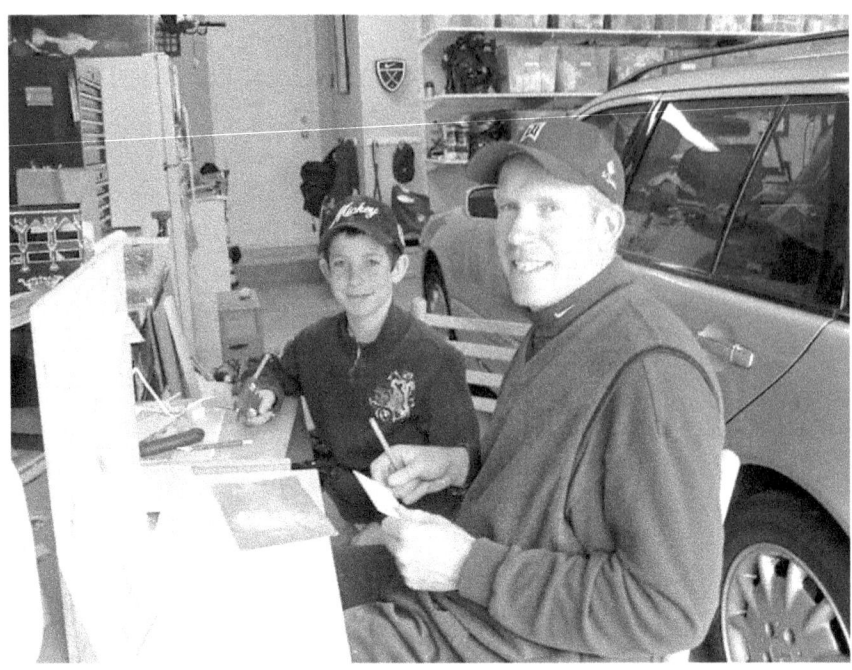

Other Books in Progress

This book is the first in a series of books for golfers. Other books currently in development include:

- Auto Maintenance for Golfers
- Home Repair for Golfers
- Amateur Surgery for Golfers
- School Projects for Golfers
- Baseball for Golfers
- Swedish Massage for Golfers
- Dentistry for Golfers
- Irish Dancing for Golfers
- Punk Music for Golfers
- Embalming for Golfers
- Bankruptcy Court for Golfers (underway already, non-fiction)
- Submarine Management for Golfers
- Palm Reading for Golfers
- Dummies for Golfers
- Writing for Golfers (Should have done that one first)

If you have any ideas for books to add to the series, please feel free to contact me through the web site. I am available for speaking engagements if you find that your preferred speaker has taken ill, and you need a stand-in at the last minute. All I need are some clean towels and some Pepto-Bismol handy.

There's a million people to thank for helping to put this book together. Don't be offended if I left you out, but maybe next time you could help a little more so I won't forget you.

Thanks

My deepest appreciation goes out to all of the people below:

Louise Blair - Props Manager, 3rd Editor
Christina Blair - 1st Editor, Talent Manager
Anthony Blair - Production Director
Thank you for everything, most especially love, enthusiasm, and support.

Patricia Blair - 2nd Editor
Best Mother and Editor in the World

Eric Isaacs, EMI Photography
for awesome original photography and for laying in the dirt to take some great shots.
(www.emiphotography.com)

Kelly Noe and Mikey the Dog
for the dog shots with the fertilizer spreader.
The lawn still has not grown back BTW

Jennifer Lewi
for the cool, legally licensed, photos
from the Associated Press
(www.apimages.org)

Tom and Hillary Sims
for allowing us to use their awesome Santa Barbara home as a backdrop for some of the photos.

Brad White, Olive Street Media
For letting me pick your brain
(www.olivestreetmedia.com)

Backword

Now that I am at the other end of the book, it may be worthwhile to talk about the journey to get here. This book started out to be a light-hearted book about golfing and gardening, but now that it is done I see it is something completely different. Sure, there's plenty of golf, and a smidgeon of material on gardening, but the book is really about Harry Potter and Disney's High School Musical (HSM). Be sure to tell your kids!

Actually there's no Harry Potter or any HSM in here at all, but J.K Rowling may buy a copy and take me golfing in Europe. I promise not to hit her with anything thicker than my thumb. If you don't get that reference, then you have not read this book all the way through. Hint: Buy another copy and start over because no two books are the same. Be sure to read the Lance Ito sidebars. I reference HSM only because my kids are big fans.

If you have read the book all the way through, then, I thank you for your patience and I hope you can appreciate my condition. Writing this book has been a wonderful experience, even if my family purchases the only copies.

Who am I kidding? My family will want free copies, probably signed, no less. Maybe Oprah will buy a copy? She lives nearby in Montecito...

Thanks again for your interest in this material. See you in the garden or the golf course sometime soon.

www.ingramcontent.com/pod-product-compliance
Lightning Source LLC
Chambersburg PA
CBHW080540170426
43195CB00016B/2628